# *Elevate*
# THE EVERYDAY

*actions and ideas to enhance the
experience of daily life*

JENNIFER MELVILLE

Copyright © 2020 Jennifer Melville

Illustrations © Elvira Silenkova

All rights reserved.

ISBN: 9798652856021

# DEDICATION

*For Jesse and Moriarty*

# CONTENTS

Introduction ........................................................................ vii

1. Elevate Your Ride ............................................................ 1
2. Connect with The Animal Kingdom ...................... 11
3. Create Your Life's Movie Soundtrack .................... 17
4. Tackle What You Are Avoiding ............................... 23
5. Dress for The Weather ............................................. 29
6. Say No to Nibbling .................................................... 37
7. Wear Blinders Doing Housework ........................... 45
8. Elevate Your Look in The Realm Of Reality ........ 51
9. Get Your Daily Dose Of Leafy Greens .................. 59
10. Make A Dreamy/ Practical List .............................. 65
11. Seek Out Skilled Beauty Advice ............................. 71
12. Scrub the Potty Mouth ............................................. 77
13. Think Outside the Big Box When Shopping ......... 83
14. Elevate More Than Just Body Parts with Exercise .... 91
15. Self Soothe in An Uplifting Manner ...................... 97
16. Acquire Intimates That Inspire ............................. 105
17. Quit Acting Your Age ............................................. 111
18. Stop Peering Over The Fence ............................... 119
19. Power Yourself with Financial Information ....... 129

20. Revisit Past Passions .................................................135
21. Find Magic in Maintenance.....................................143
22. Act Now..................................................................151

A Note from The Author.............................................157
About the Author.........................................................159

# INTRODUCTION

Hello! I am so happy you picked up this little book of mine. It represents the final product of an exciting personal journey for me. Dipping my toe into the world of writing and self-publishing has allowed me to explore and share a topic I am passionate about; seeking ways to elevate and beautify the experience of daily life. We only get one shot at our physical existence on this earth, so why not make the very best of it? There is certainly a lot of pain and sadness in life, but there is also great joy and beauty. Sometimes we need a gentle nudge to take notice of the sliver of magic and possibility sitting right in front of our noses. Finding ways to walk through our days deliberately and with thought and care for our own happiness can elevate all areas of life. Even the most mundane and banal of life's moments and experiences can be infused with uplifting joy, beauty and serenity.

A professional accountant by trade, I have always found pleasure in approaching my life with an analytical mind. I enjoy stepping back and examining the various aspects of my life as *systems*. Just as I used to evaluate the flow and efficiency of my clients' accounting systems, it made sense to adopt the same approach at home and in my personal life. I am constantly tweaking the little areas of my life, seeking out ways to elevate the experience of living and reduce annoyances. My goal is not to operate in such an efficient manner that life feels rigid and inflexible, governed by a long list of unattainable expectations and high standards. I like to seek ways that make my days run more smoothly, but always keeping a pleasant, peaceful and uplifting approach in mind.

These are my own musings based on personal experience and observation. I have been exploring the topic of improving my life and raising the bar in specific areas for over twenty years. Living well and elevating your life is a journey, not a destination! I certainly did not implement all these ideas in a month! They evolved slowly and many of them are still a work in progress for me. I encourage you to read these thoughts and reflections with a light heart and spirit (no pressure and no perfectionism). Have fun incorporating those aspects of the book that spark your interest and suit your lifestyle. You could choose just one that you wish to focus on, or maybe a handful that appeal to you.

Some of these ideas are quick snappers, and others involve a lot more time, thought and effort. Most of the concepts I discuss are not groundbreaking or earth shattering in nature. They are topics many of us explore and revisit often in our daily lives. My purpose in sharing my experiences and opinions is to *inspire* and *remind*. I hope to inspire you to adopt practices that perhaps you had not previously considered and offer some simple actions you can start immediately to elevate your life. Perhaps many of my suggestions are already ingrained in your daily life. I hope my reminders motivate you to keep up the great work or offer little tidbits to fine-tune and improve your efforts.

So, please sit back in a comfy chair with a cup of tea and notebook in hand! Perhaps you will read the book from start to finish, or scan the table of contents to choose a topic that triggers your curiosity. Enjoy the process of analyzing your own life and exploring methods to elevate your everyday!

# 1

# ELEVATE YOUR RIDE

I spend a lot more time in my vehicle than I would like to admit. As a mother of two active teen boys, I can often be found chauffeuring my brood to all corners of the city. I have jokingly referred to my circular trips from home to Point A and B as my "road trip to nowhere". We live in a rural community, so even a carton of milk requires a jaunt in the car.

I have resigned myself to the fact that my chauffeuring career will carry on for the next few years, and I am actually quite content in my present situation. This is the reality of my current season in life and my role as a mother. It is a beautiful and rewarding time, where I am able to raise and support my children through the precarious teen years. Driving them all over creation just happens to be one of the support systems they need right now!

I used to be that frazzled mother of toddlers with a car that smelled like sour milk and was littered with half-eaten sandwiches, untold thousands of Cheerios and piles of junk mail and food wrappers. We once discovered an unidentified plant that had sprouted under the passenger seat! Maybe you can relate to the feeling of just giving up on your vehicle? Back then, I drove a very old beat up Volvo my father had given us. It had been our family car growing up and still had a few good years left, so I was very appreciative of his kind gesture. I knew I had given up all hope for my vehicle the day I decided to use it to transport a load of seaweed home in the trunk. (It was destined for my garden beds.) I placed the seaweed in garbage bags, but apparently, I didn't secure them adequately. As we headed home from the beach, a colony of sand fleas escaped the trunk and swarmed the interior of the vehicle! Thankfully, that car was on its very last legs and was soon sold for a few hundred dollars. That wasn't the only bad decision I made. We once adopted a couple of lambs, and in my wisdom, I figured it was a good idea to transport them home in the back of my SUV. It was a two-hour car ride back to our house. I will let you use your imagination on what the vehicle smelled like when we pulled into the garage.

If any of this sounds familiar to you, I speak from personal experience, there is hope! I have since changed my attitude about my vehicle and have elevated the driving experience. I no longer dread climbing into a cluttered car, but rather feel a sense of calm as I turn on the ignition and pull out of the driveway. I recommend you view the interior of your car as an extension of your home environment. Like a tidy home, a tidy vehicle makes me feel calm, in control and pulled together.

Yes, in my dream life I would be zipping around town in a cute little Euro-chic hatchback, the perfect grocery-getter for me to maneuver my way into tight parking spots and down narrow one-way streets. Instead, my current ride is a ten-year-old battered SUV. Its tires are so large and rugged, I literally have to hoist my short frame into the driver's seat. It suits our family's current season perfectly and is often packed to the gunnels with snowboards, sailing gear and sweaty adolescents. Although many of us might prefer a lush and plush driving experience behind the wheel of a luxury vehicle, you can find ways to elevate your current situation (even if you are driving a $400 ancient Volvo).

Since I spend so much time behind the wheel, it is rewarding to find ways to elevate the driving experience. The biggest, and most important step in my view, is to do a deep-clean of the interior. This might be a bigger task for some than others! I usually tackle deep-cleans on sunny days where I can park it in the driveway and turn on the tunes while I drag out the vacuum cleaner and a bucket of warm water. I start by removing every single thing from the vehicle, including the mats and contents of the console and glove compartment (and of course the trash and miscellaneous random objects). You might want to hire someone to detail your car if you don't have the time or energy to do this first deep-clean on your own. Depending on the state of your car, it could be money well spent. I promise you, after this dreaded task is done, you will feel like a new person every time you climb behind the wheel.

I am not going to get into a play-by-play of "how to clean your car", but I do want to comment on my experience with traditional interior car cleaning products. I find them extremely strong and unpleasantly scented. I usually wipe down the dusty interior with a bucket of warm soapy water (I use unscented dish soap) that I infuse with a few drops of lavender oil. This seems to tackle the job of cleaning things adequately, while adding a pleasant, inspiring and relaxing scent. Lavender has always been a favorite of mine because it reminds me of my trips to the South of France. I also stash a few sachets of dried lavender under the seats. These do wonders at combating the nasty scent of sporting gear and wet dog! Do you have a favorite scent you would enjoy being greeted by when you open your car? Nice choices might be orange, rosemary, pine or peppermint.

Once your car is sparkling clean, implementing a few easy steps will keep it that way going forward. It involves a bit of self-discipline, but I find that driving around in my fresh, clean vehicle motivates me to stick to maintenance habits.

I have a policy that everyone needs to remove their belongings from the car upon exiting. This includes my own personal belongings, mail and shopping bags. The key is, it also includes my *children's* school bags, gum wrappers and random pieces of clothing or sports gear. (They have a strange habit of stripping off their shoes and socks upon entering the vehicle.) When this task is completed consistently, it is easy to stay on top of things. You will never find yourself with a heap in the backseat again. This takes full participation from others and yes, there may be a lot of nagging involved if you have a family. I keep a small plastic trash bag in the backseat to encourage compliance, and it seems to help with my younger passengers.

I generally keep the radio off in the vehicle unless I am specifically looking for a news update or information on traffic delays. Most conventional radio stations have nothing to offer except blaring advertisements. I like pop songs just as much as anybody, so if I am craving music of this nature, I will simply pull up a playlist on my phone. I have many driving playlists (or soundtracks as I refer to them) custom tailored for my many moods. Again, sometimes I have an appetite for uplifting pop, other times I prefer something calming and classical. I also listen to podcasts if I am embarking on a longer drive.

More often than not, I enjoy the delicious sound of silence while driving! Sitting behind the wheel offers a rare opportunity for me to have alone time, so I really do savour the lack of noise. If I do have passengers in tow, the quiet allows us to connect and have a meaningful conversation. After school pick-up time with the boys is often an opportunity for deep discussion about their days. Alone in the car together, free from distractions, we have engaged in some of our best and most honest discussions.

I love the *idea* of a "no eating in the car" policy. Again, the concept appeals to me, but it is just not practical for our family. If it were just me buzzing around town in my chic little car, this rule would not be a problem. Hungry teen boys seem to require constant refuelling. A full meal before soccer practice is usually followed by a snack on the way to the field. The trash bag in the backseat helps (as long as there is adequate nagging to actually use it). I drive the family car, but my husband has a vehicle that is almost exclusively used for his commute to work. Other than his morning coffee, he refrains from munching in his car. Let's just say his daily ride is much cleaner than mine and as a result, requires much less regular maintenance.

Routine upkeep of your fresh interior is the key to making your goal of a clean car manageable. I keep a package of wipes in the console. During idle time in the car, such as waiting at school pick-ups, I give the dash a quick wipe down. Doing this once or twice a week does wonders. I perform a deeper clean where I shake the mats, vacuum and do a thorough wipe down of the interior once a month. My husband's vehicle requires this type of attention less frequently. The whole process takes less than half an hour, and I have a big vehicle! If someone in my house is looking for money (and what teen isn't?) this chore is often contracted out to one of my sons.

There is nothing fun about running on exhaust fumes. It is anxiety provoking to watch that big red empty indicator light up when you are nowhere near a service station. Why not save yourself the stress and avoid this situation as much as possible? I fill up my car on a regular weekly schedule, even if it is not running very low. Adopting this routine only takes a few minutes and prevents the worry of running out of gas.

Is your glove compartment a junk drawer like mine was? It contained all the important papers, but clearing it out unearthed a hodgepodge of items, from a pair of socks to an old tennis ball. I compiled the important documents, such as the proof of insurance and the registration, and placed them in an envelope, along with the car manual. That is all that resides in the glove box today. Not long after my deep-clean, I was pulled over for speeding (for the first time in almost thirty years as a licensed driver!) Instead of rifling through a messy glove compartment, I was able to efficiently pull out the necessary documents for the police officer. My sense of satisfaction for being so organized helped soothe the sting of embarrassment and the pricey ticket! Yes, a clean and organized car even elevated my experience of a driving infraction!

## ELEVATING ACTIONS:

- View your car as an extension of your home and a space that you would like to feel calm, relaxed and organized.
- If it is needed, do a deep-clean of your vehicle to kickstart your new clean car policy.
- Empty your vehicle every time you return home and enlist other members of the family to do the same.
- Create your own "road trip to nowhere" playlists to inspire, uplift or relax you. Drive in silence if your soul needs it.
- Avoid eating in your car as much as possible. Keep a small trash bag handy to collect wrappers and other waste. Encourage all family members to actually *use* the trash bag!
- Store a container of wipes in the console so they are handy to do a quick wipe down during idle time.
- Choose a scent that pleases you and add a few drops of this essential oil to your cleaning bucket for an uplifting jolt each time you open the door.
- Tuck scented sachets of dried flowers under the car seats to combat unpleasant odors.

- Reserve your glove compartment for important manuals and documents so they are easily accessible when needed.
- Fill the gas tank weekly so you are never running on empty.
- Set up a monthly maintenance system or schedule for both the interior and exterior of your vehicle. Enlist the help of other members of the household.

# 2

# CONNECT WITH THE ANIMAL KINGDOM

All of you animal-lovers out there will agree with me on this one, critters both big and small can enrich and elevate your life. Adopting a pet is certainly not for everyone and should never be made as a rash decision. Before taking on such a long-term commitment, it is really important to assess whether you can provide a pet with the care and attention it needs, and whether it would suit your lifestyle and financial position.

With all that being said, if you believe a pet might fit nicely into your current situation, an animal companion can certainly add an uplifting and rewarding dimension to your life. Our family recently adopted an adorable toy poodle puppy named Coco. Since he has come into my life, every day still feels like Christmas morning! His presence around the house gives me a feeling of constant companionship and he provides the whole family with endless entertainment. If I find myself in a sour mood, cuddle or play time with Coco lightens my spirits. In this very moment, he is curled up in a ball, faithfully positioned at my feet. If you already own a pet, I am sure you can relate to how much of an abundance of joy they add to your life.

Maybe you have a number of reasons a pet would not suit your lifestyle. Perhaps you travel regularly, have mobility issues, or work outside the home for extended periods of time. For those of you in this position, I invite you to think outside the box! There are a number of ways you might be able to bring the pleasure of animal camaraderie into your life.

For most people, dogs and cats are the first critters that come to mind when they hear the word pet. Adopting either of these is certainly a big decision, not to be taken lightly. There are, however, other lower-maintenance companions out there that might suit your lifestyle. In addition to our pooch, my sons have three beautiful rosy bourke parakeets. Our bourkes are sweet, quiet birds and their presence really adds a warm atmosphere to our home. Their cage sits in the corner of our living room and I am entertained by their soft and sweet chirping throughout the day. One of them even learned to say his name, which is quite charming! Cleaning and feeding are very easy and simple tasks; in fact my son is in charge of these duties. They are the type of pet you can leave for a few days with the food and water bowls topped up. When our family travels on a longer vacation, we hire a local child to pop in and care for them every few days. If you are interested in birds, I encourage you to do some research. Many large parrots and parakeets command *a lot* of attention and work, but some of the smaller ones are great for beginners or those seeking simpler care requirements.

Do you adore felines, but just can't commit? Maybe you have always been a dog-lover but find yourself in a season of life unsuitable for a pet. Again, thinking outside the box opens opportunities to enjoy the company of animals with a less onerous commitment. Maybe you have a favorite neighborhood dog you bump into each day on your morning walk. You could volunteer to pet sit now and then. Is there an elderly person in the community who might appreciate your offering of a free dog walking service? I have incorporated these ideas into my life in the past and they have proven to be rewarding experiences. As a child, I pet sat regularly for my dog crush Rover who lived down the street. Not only was it a way to earn income, but I cherished the time I got to spend with him alone. Both of my children participated in a program at a local shelter where they read to cats each week. This was a win-win situation! The cats got snuggles and attention, and my children practised their reading in a non-threatening environment with a safe, cuddly audience.

This next idea is one that has brought a great deal of enjoyment to all members of my family. Could you find a spot outside your home for a birdfeeder? We keep our feeders stocked year-round. The view out my living room window this morning included chickadees, juncos, goldfinches and a mourning dove. These feathered friends elevate my morning tea with their songs and vibrant plumage. You really don't need much space for this! My one-hundred-year-old great aunt installed a suction cup birdfeeder on the outside of her nursing home window!

In my youth, I attended horseback riding camps every summer. Owning a horse of my own was always a childhood dream, but never a possibility. Maybe it is time to rekindle an old hobby or passion such as riding, where you can interact with these majestic creatures once again.

My sister took up wildlife photography as a hobby, and over the years she has captured some astonishing and breathtaking images of creatures big and small. By sharing her stunning photos with her family, friends and community, the enjoyment of her wildlife sightings extends far beyond her camera lens. She was even awarded a runner up prize in the annual wildlife photography competition run by Canadian Geographic!

There really are countless creative ways to interact with the animal kingdom. Finding one that suits your personality and lifestyle can enrich daily life with joy, unconditional love and companionship.

## **ELEVATING ACTIONS:**

- Consider adding an animal companion to your life to reap the joyful benefits pets offer.
- Explore and research lower maintenance pet options that might be more suitable to your lifestyle.
- Think outside the box on how you could enrich and elevate your life with animals without the commitment. Volunteering to pet sit or dog walk might be a rewarding option.
- Install a bird feeder and marvel at the feathered friends that will visit you each day. If you feed them, they will come!
- Consider ways you can combine current or old hobbies with your love of animals.

# 3

# CREATE YOUR LIFE'S MOVIE SOUNDTRACK

Music has always played an influential role in my life, even though I can't sing or play an instrument. I certainly do not come from a "musical family". My own musical training consists of two years of agonising piano lessons, for which I never practised or demonstrated any interest. I actually created recordings of scales which I played loudly on a tape recorder during practice time. This way I was able hide in the basement reading a novel, while my trusting mother listened to the scales floating up to the kitchen. (Sorry Mom!) Imagine my delight when a broken arm in grade five finally allowed me to quit the dreaded weekly sessions!

I also experimented briefly with guitar lessons in my early twenties. I actually felt great hope for my musical future after the first lesson, when my teacher informed me that I possessed a rare genetic gift known in guitar circles as the "cobbler's thumb". Apparently, my "gift" did not extend beyond my double-jointed digit. He quickly changed his opinion of me when I admitted to having never heard of Gordon Lightfoot. If you are not from Canada, you can be forgiven for not recognizing this name, but I was sternly informed that he was our country's most iconic folk artist and was an esteemed Officer of the Order of Canada. Ouch! The lessons were never quite the same after this admission of ignorance. I also never mastered anything beyond the chords of C, G and E minor. (For the record, you can play quite a few tunes with this limited repertoire.)

Despite all this, I just know that music moves me and elevates my life experiences. It has the power to lift my spirits, soothe my soul, ignite my energy and even fuel my anger.

I have had a love affair with movie soundtracks from an early age. Growing up, *Annie* was probably my favorite. I spent hours in my basement re-enacting every scene from that movie with my dolls and stuffed animals. I actually used to blast *It's the Hard Knock Life* on my record player when doing my chores!

If *your* life were a movie, imagine what soundtrack music would be playing in the background. Brainstorm ideas for the mood and tone you would like your soundtrack to convey. View your life as a series of various scenes and settings. What musical accompaniment could enhance these experiences? My scenes include: my morning run, going for a walk, puttering around the house, cooking a meal, heavy duty cleaning, working at my computer desk, relaxing in bed, having a bath, dozing on the couch and zipping around the city in my car to run errands. Each of these scenes can often be elevated by adding music to the experience. My running soundtrack is full of energetic beats that push me to pick up my pace or power up a hill. (As cheesy as this sounds, I will admit to playing *Chariots of Fire* on occasion.) My kitchen soundtrack is sometimes French café music that helps motivate me to find joy in the process of making a meal instead of approaching it as a chore. While relaxing in bed or having a bath, I might opt for something more spa and Zen-like to soothe my mind and transport me to a blissful state. Background music can be particularly uplifting in situations that feel hum-drum, boring or uninspiring (think cleaning the bathroom).

Next time you watch a movie that inspires you, start paying attention to the background music. Make a list of some of your favorite feel-good movies. Have fun re-watching them and take note of particular songs you enjoy or inspiring moments when the background score elevates the experience. The music from the movie *Amélie* is one of my favorites and sets the mood perfectly when I want to transport myself to the streets of Paris. I sometimes play it on a walk through my neighborhood and imagine myself sauntering through a much more exotic location than the same old streets. Other favorites of mine include *A Good Year, Forrest Gump, Sleepless in Seattle, P.S. I Love You and Braveheart.* I adore David Foster's work (fellow Canadian)! *The Love Theme from St. Elmo's Fire* is a preferred go-to when I find myself in a sentimental mood. Have fun exploring what inspires *you*.

With the technology we have available, creating your soundtracks is so much easier than in the past. (Remember those old mixed-tapes and the cumbersome process we went through to create them?) I really do prefer the word soundtrack to playlist. It sounds more fun and inspirational to view your life as a story or movie being played out with you as the main character. Once you have your soundtracks created, use them regularly to elevate the experiences of your daily life. Play them in the car, on your walk, while sipping your morning coffee and while scrubbing the toilet!

I often use my headphones in the house if my family is home and everyone is going about their business. This escape mechanism can come in handy when I am trying to drown out annoying background noise (which in my case is the sound of skateboard wheels rolling back and forth on the plywood half pipe my son built in the basement).

Here is a bit of a funny story where a soundtrack handily served the purpose of distraction for me. My family was on a vacation in the South of France a few years ago. We had a home base at an Airbnb and spent our days sightseeing and travelling to the various surrounding villages. It was time to head home, but when my husband turned on the ignition, an internal car alarm was activated. Although the car was functioning, the audio and navigation systems were down, and the irritating alarm persisted. He tried everything to shut it off, to no avail. We decided all we could do was drive back to our villa and call the car rental agency for support. All the while, we were suspicious that one of our children had flicked a switch or pressed a button, but lips were tight, and admissions were not forthcoming. The drive back felt like a scene from *National Lampoon's European Vacation*, winding our way through the picturesque French countryside with the alarm grating on my nerves more and more with each passing moment. What a great time to pull out my dreamy French girl soundtrack and lose myself in another universe. I listened to the soundtrack from *A Good Year*, which was actually filmed in the region of Provence we were visiting. It drowned out the car alarm quite nicely and allowed me to focus my attention on the scenery (clearly elevating the present moment). When we arrived home, someone finally admitted to opening the door to the gas tank, so the problem was solved!

## **ELEVATING ACTIONS:**

- Inspire yourself by viewing your life as a series of scenes from a movie with you as star of the show!
- Make a list of themes you would like to incorporate into your life. This list might include words like inspiring, energising, soothing, relaxing…etc.
- Have fun exploring movie music (and just general music). Re-watching favorite films from the past is a great place to start.
- Create a series of soundtracks (playlists) that focus on the themes you identified that you would like to incorporate into the movie of your life.
- Find ways to integrate your soundtracks regularly into your day to day activities.
- Keep headphones handy for those moments when distracting yourself from an annoying situation would be helpful. I use wireless headphones and find them very convenient to use while doing chores around the house.

# 4

# TACKLE WHAT YOU ARE AVOIDING

I am a firm believer that what we are avoiding often turns out to be what we need the most. There have been so many times I have found myself pleasantly surprised by trying something I had labelled as, "not for me". That's not to say it hasn't gone in the other direction, but I think it supports a case for trying new things now and then, even if you don't think it suits you. You may just discover that the story you created in your head is holding you back from something that could enhance or elevate your life!

As I mentioned, I have a number of personal experiences that support this view, and I am guessing you might too! Back in my early twenties, at the peak of an unhealthy lifestyle, I was feeling frustrated with my lack of success in establishing a consistent exercise routine. I was travelling a great deal and working long hours at an accounting firm. There was never any consistency to my evening schedule. My boyfriend (now husband) had just started going to the gym at 6 a.m. to make sure he got his workouts in before the unpredictable hectic day began. When he suggested I do the same, I baulked! I *loved* sleeping in. I could *never* get up that early to workout. Well, it turns out I could, I did, and I have stuck with my morning exercise routine for over twenty years. I am at a point where I rely on my early workouts to jump start my day. It is as natural a routine as brushing my teeth. Pushing through that mental block set me up on a path towards wellness. I dropped over fifteen pounds, made incredible friends at the gym, and developed some really healthy life-long habits. The only thing holding me back was myself, and the story I created that I wasn't a morning person.

I *hate* running.

I could *never* give up dairy.

I will *never* get a dog. They are too much work.

I *can't* meditate.

All of these statements turned out to be false. By ignoring the voice in my head and turning each one of them from a perceived negative to an actual positive, I improved my life significantly, elevating the experience of my day to day.

I encourage you to take time to reflect on what you might be avoiding in life. Brainstorm a list of all the things you dream of in the back of your mind, but have convinced yourself are not possible. Take an inventory of activities you have labelled as "not your cup of tea". Examine and question the arguments behind your reasoning. Why not challenge yourself to put your stories and theories to the test? You might confirm your suspicions, or you might find yourself pleasantly surprised. Do you hear yourself making statements such as: "I hate exercise. I can't draw. I'm not creative. I'm not flexible enough to do yoga….etc." ? Are you willing to open the door just a crack to peek inside at the possibilities?

I like to take the approach of dipping my toe in the water first. It feels a little less intimidating and more achievable to wade in slowly. I applied this strategy to all of the items on my list (except the dog! I took the plunge when it came to my puppy). When I started running, I tried it on the treadmill first, in increments of ten minutes. That way I wouldn't find myself stranded far from home. This progressed to running outside with a lovely new friend I met at the gym. Two years later, we completed our first marathon together! It turns out it wasn't running I hated. What I disliked was being out of shape and gasping for air. Once I worked my way up, I came to not just love running, but *need* it. It infuses my life with joy, solitude, challenge, physical fitness and energy.

Maybe you have heard about the benefits of mediation, but just don't think you could sit still enough to do it. I started a program that guided me through a baby-step approach, beginning with just one minute a day! It is an area I am still exploring. I am up to 20-minute sessions a few times a week, but I am definitely experiencing some of the benefits mindfulness has to offer.

A couple of years ago I decided to experiment with a plant-based diet. My husband scoffed at the idea at first. He claimed that being a big, athletic and active male, there was no way his body could be sustained by just eating plant products. I was so impressed when he gave it a try and it turns out he hasn't looked back since he made the switch.

Why not take a good hard look at what you are avoiding in life? What do you have to lose? Certainly, you may find out that you were right all along. You are in fact not interested in ball room dancing! But maybe you will find out you were *wrong* all along!

## ELEVATING ACTIONS:

- Brainstorm a list of things you notice yourself avoiding.
- Make note when you turn your nose up at something that is "not your cup of tea". Ask yourself if you could open your mind to it.
- Start with slow and small steps, easing yourself into new activities and situations.

- Find inspiration in your successes. Remind yourself of situations where trying something you were avoiding turned out to benefit you. Use this as motivation when faced with the next challenge.

# 5

# DRESS FOR THE WEATHER

Do you ever feel like the weather is dragging you down and cramping your style? Is there one particular season that leaves you feeling the most deflated? Nothing quite sucks the joy out of my time spent outdoors than being ill-dressed for the weather. Whether I am freezing to death (most often the case), soaked to the bone or melting, such physical discomfort has a way of dragging me down. Recognizing this in myself, I decided to put some thought into how to brave the elements and elevate my day to day life.

I live in Canada, and though this majestic country has many positive qualities, in my opinion the climate is not one of them. I do love our four distinct seasons, and the beauty that each has to offer. The problem is that winter seems to drag on for what feels like an eternity. Since I live by the sea, the cold ocean temperature causes winter weather to stick around until practically the first day of summer! My ideal world would be one that alternates between summer and fall, with a token snow day thrown in for Christmas. I guess I am a "Goldilocks" when it comes to weather. I like things just right; not too cold, not too hot. Anything outside my comfortable temperature range and I either start wilting (rarely) or slipping into hibernation mode (often).

The long, dark winter months are definitely the most challenging for me. This generally spans from November to mid-April (or later). I realize I am whining, but the truth is, winter cramps my style! I would enter the cooler months with a sense of anticipation and excitement about my carefully curated fall/winter wardrobe, only to be dispirited when the frigid, wintry conditions arrived. There is nothing elegant or chic about scaling a snow bank in your nice leather-heeled boots to drop a quarter in the parking meter. (Losing your boot in said snowbank adds to the unglamorous nature of this experience.) I found myself always feeling contracted, hunched over and miserable when I went outside.

Since I'm not moving anytime soon, I needed to find a way to embrace the cold weather. Looking forward to it was a stretch. I was searching for a way to live the winter months in comfort, grace and a dash of style. One approach I took was loading the woodstove to create an inferno-like atmosphere in our home. My husband often complains about my thermometer reading of a toasty twenty-six degrees Celsius. This suits *me* just fine, but it doesn't help my situation when I have to venture outdoors.

I wanted to feel elevated when I walked out the door, instead of shrunken by the chill.

I realized I needed to let go of the idea of the fall/winter wardrobe that I had read about in so many books and blogs. What I wear in the fall months looks very different from the winter. Fall days are pleasantly crisp, but also very often comfortably warm. The fall season is most likely my favorite time for dressing. Layering with cozy scarves and cardigans is fun and can really elevate a look. Dresses, skirts, clogs, booties and blouses are all included in my autumn wardrobe plan.

None of these items are in my winter wardrobe. It sounds a bit drastic, but I have found a formula that works for me in the coldest of months. Almost all my tops are cashmere turtleneck sweaters. I have a nice collection of colors (blue, green, grey, black, camel) so I don't get bored. On the bottom it is always a slim fitting pant, which is most often skinny jeans in black, dark blue or grey. Anything with a wide leg is off the table as they do not tuck nicely into a winter boot. Skirts and dresses, even with tights on, just don't cut it for me. I wear a silk camisole underneath my sweaters for extra warmth and this seems to keep me happy and comfortable around our home. This has been my winter uniform for the last three years and it feels perfect for my lifestyle and environment.

Do you remember the days of junior high, when looking cool took priority over everything else? I try to shake off the "bad mother" feeling when I drop my teenage son off for school in sub-zero temperatures with just a thin hoodie and sneakers on. He braved an entire Canadian winter without wearing a hat, gloves, jacket or snow boots! Well, my own days of junior high are over, and I have come to realize you don't need to sacrifice style for comfort.

I took some time to research and invest in warm, practical *and* stylish winter outerwear. I have a navy wool peacoat for mild days and a longer black down coat for the frigid ones. My favorite leather-soled booties retire to storage once the snow starts to fly. My rugged-soled, shearling-lined leather boots that I wear on a daily basis are really attractive, but also keep me warm and dry. (I have successfully scaled a snow bank in them while maintaining my style and poise.) They are made by Frye and I found them on eBay for a good price during the off-season. I have a small collection of fun accessories; cozy gloves, scarves and hats (we call them *toques* in Canada). Dare I say I actually look forward to wearing my winter attire? It seems having winter-wear that I really love somehow makes the season more bearable.

After snow comes rain of course. My coastal climate definitely includes a lot of cold, wet weather. Having a raincoat that you really love definitely helps make the wet weather less miserable. I found a stylish but fairly inexpensive rain coat that hits me just above the knee. Having a longer coat is the key to staying comfortable, as it keeps my legs dry. There is nothing worse than soaking wet jeans glued to your legs. Paired with my tall rubber boots, I usually feel like I am ready to face the day when it rains. Puddle jumping could actually be an option!

Hot weather is something I don't have a lot of experience with, though I know many of you do! We tend to have a two-week period of hot humid weather each summer. No matter how sticky and sweaty I feel, you will never hear me complain about the heat! I love the free and easy feeling that comes with summer weather and I wear dresses or skirts almost exclusively during this time. I opt for short and loose cotton or linen tunics that don't cling to my body and give me room to move.

Since I hit my forties, I have become hyper-aware of the damaging effects of the sun on our skin. If I had a time machine, I would go back and tell my foolish youthful self to wear sunscreen! Can you believe I used to lie out and tan with my body slathered in Mazola corn oil? Insane, I know! My summer survival kit now includes a straw hat. I love the fact that I am protecting myself from the sun and heat, but also elevating my style. Straw hats scream vacation vibe to me, which definitely lifts my mood. They should not be reserved for beach days! I also have one good pair of oversized sunglasses that not only protect my eyes, but polish the look (think "Jackie O").

Do you have your own weather woes? Is there one particular season that leaves you feeling the most deflated? I recommend contemplating ways to elevate your experience of that season, instead of dreading it. Make this a fun and inspiring project. Motivate yourself by imagining how chic and pulled together you will look in your outerwear or accessories, ready to face anything that mother nature throws at you. I set up a Pinterest board specifically for winter outerwear. I did this during the summer, so I had plenty of time to plan ahead. If you enjoy snagging a deal on sites like eBay, buying seasonal items in the off-season is a great approach.

Maybe you live in an area where the rain is relentless for months on end. A really great raincoat that you *love* could be a life changer! Maybe a fun and colorful umbrella might do the trick. A stylish waterproof handbag could come in handy in keeping your belongings dry. Your leather one might be best saved for dryer periods.

Are you the person running to the nearest building to be saved by the air-conditioning? A small collection of fashionable hats and sunglasses might infuse those sweltering days with a touch of joy (even though you will likely still be melting). What cool and stylish outfits could you look forward to wearing when the sun is blazing? Maybe a chic water bottle could be your new go-to accessory to get you through the day. What tips and tricks could you incorporate into your life to make the heat a little more bearable? (Psst....I carry an extra pair of undies in my purse just in case I need a fresh pick me up!)

## **ELEVATING ACTIONS:**

- Dress for both style and comfort when it comes to the weather.
- Identify the weather or season you feel challenged by and put some thought into what could elevate the experience for you.
- Have fun gathering inspiration on outerwear or accessories that could protect you from the elements *and* enhance your style.
- Plan ahead to approach this task with plenty of time to prepare yourself for the challenging weather. When it finally arrives, you will be ready to face it with a contented smile!

# 6

# SAY NO TO NIBBLING

Mindless snacking is a tough one for all of us to tackle. Food is never far from our fingertips and we are constantly bombarded with temptations. Our innate yearning for fat, sugar and salt does not serve us well in a society that offers these enticing treats in abundance.

I grew up with a very health-conscious mother. She studied nutrition in university, so it is no surprise that she put a lot of effort into providing our family with nourishing meals. Once I left her nest, however, my eating habits went off the rails! My university diet consisted of pizza, garlic fingers, french fries, cinnamon toast, instant noodles, and just to throw something healthy in the mix, iceberg lettuce with blue cheese dressing. Dinner time was never complete without a trip to the all-you-can-eat ice cream buffet at the meal hall.

My bad habits followed me as I embarked on a career in public accounting. I put in very long hours at the firm and regularly used treats as a reward to get through the work days. Mid-morning breaks always included a mammoth muffin from the coffee shop in the lobby. The afternoon slump often involved another trip to the same shop to pick up a daily dose of warm and gooey chocolate chip cookies, fresh out of the oven. (I got so that I could time my arrival perfectly.) After hours I would find myself at the office vending machine, guzzling down a Pepsi for a sugar and caffeine hit. "Busy season" was the worst, as the combination of consecutive months of working long hours and unhealthy eating encouraged a disastrous pattern of behaviour.

I actually don't recognize the person I just described as myself, because I have come such a long way in elevating my eating habits. Over the years I have done a complete 360 on the way I approach food. It has been twenty years since the days of hovering over the vending machine. Ironically, nutrition is now one of my passions. Last spring I completed a certificate in plant-based nutrition offered through eCornell. These days, instead of craving junk food, I have an appetite for learning new information and tweaking my diet to suit my season in life and my changing body.

I am very thoughtful about what foods I put in my body. That being said, I am human, and I still have an affinity for salt, fat and sugar! Unhealthy snack foods are tempting for all of us and they are designed to be that way! In fact, even healthy snack foods can lead you away from your goals if you are eating mindlessly and consuming more calories than your body needs. Almonds are certainly a health food, but if you sit down and scarf back half a cup (which is so easy to do), you've just consumed over four hundred calories. I had to laugh the day I found my son in front of the television with an empty bag of trail mix I had just picked up at the bulk store. Just out of curiosity I calculated the number of calories he had consumed in one snacking session. It came in at a whopping six thousand! (3500 calories=1pound) His growing teen body incinerated those calories instantly. I can't say mine would have done the same thing!

I am not perfect with my eating, and I don't really strive to be. I have implemented little tricks to keep *mindless* snacking at bay. I emphasize the word mindless, because I think this is where we run into trouble. A planned healthy mid-morning snack of apple slices and almond butter is nourishing and energy boosting. A planned treat of a small slice of cake to celebrate a special occasion can be uplifting and satisfying to the soul. An unplanned, mindless late-night snack of potato chips straight from the bag is unhealthy, and energy draining. Do you ever feel *good* after eating chips?

One suggestion I often hear is to keep junk food out of the house completely. This is one of those instances where I love the *idea*, but the concept does not always translate well into real life. If you live alone, this makes perfect sense! When you live with others, you can't always control what comes through the door. Halloween comes to mind!

Back when my children were sweet, innocent and gullible, I created a mythical character known as the "Green Pumpkin". The boys were instructed to leave their bulging treat bags on their doorknobs if they wanted to receive a very special surprise. On Halloween night, the Green Pumpkin would magically descend upon our home to exchange their candy for an exciting gift! Intrigued, they fell for it. I picked up a few dinky cars at Walmart and made the swap. The treats headed to the office with my husband and my kids were completely ecstatic about the new toys. This only lasted a couple of years. Eventually the Green Pumpkin started handing out twenty-dollar bills. He finally gave up and took off with the Tooth Fairy, never to be seen again. These days, Halloween night is spent sorting, gobbling and bartering treats. The temptations sit around the house for weeks!

I have come up with a few tricks to keep me on track with my eating. I have an expression in my house that I use quite often; "the kitchen is closed". This is basically a message to my family that I am no longer on duty to help out in the kitchen. If they would like an evening snack, they are welcome to it, but it is a self-serve operation. With teens in the house, I try to keep the fridge and cupboards stocked with quick and healthy items. These might include baby carrots and hummus, trail mix or pre-cut fruit. There are definitely treats in the mix of options. My children have growing bodies, so I would certainly never encourage a no-snacking policy for them. Their caloric needs are through the roof at the moment, their stomachs seemingly endless pits.

I am in an opposite position to the teen males in my household. As a short female in her mid-forties, my caloric needs are actually on the decline! I use the "kitchen is closed" mentality on myself as well. Once dinner is finished and the dishes are done, the kitchen is closed to me. For some reason, the sight of nice clean countertops helps with the delivery of this message. When the kitchen is closed, I'm done for the day. I have eaten healthfully for the day, I'm not hungry and I should feel satisfied. Evening cravings are just that, cravings, not hunger.

Another evening trick I use is brushing and flossing my teeth right after dinner, instead of waiting for bedtime. This is actually really effective because if I am going to go to all that bother of flossing, I don't want to ruin my hard work with nibbling.

Sometimes I find myself running errands longer than expected. To prevent myself from falling prey to unhealthy drive-thru options, I keep snacks on hand in my car console. My emergency stash of nuts and healthy bars is there if I need it and usually beats whatever else is available on the road.

Plan your healthy snacks and savour them! Choose foods that elevate and nourish you and that you really enjoy. If you take the time to think ahead and plan a mid-afternoon snack, it is much more likely to be a healthy choice. I often opt for a small handful of nuts and seeds and a piece of fruit, or veggies and hummus. If I am really hungry, I might make a small smoothie to keep me going until my next meal.

If I find myself wanting to give in to emotional eating, I seek out a warm, comforting drink instead. Sometimes when I want to eat a plate of chocolate chip cookies, I am really just craving an emotional boost of pleasure that the taste of the cookies will provide. Warm tea with soy milk is my comfort drink. Cozying up with a cup of this beverage often provides the soothing emotional lift I'm looking for. What is your comfort drink? Maybe it's a coffee, or a refreshing glass of water with lemon. Water can feel really nourishing and kind to the soul.

Don't deprive yourself of your favorite treats! My current indulgence of choice is one peanut butter chocolate truffle each day after lunch with my tea. I just have one and it seems to be all I need or want. It satisfies my craving for chocolate and feels so decadent in the moment, that I never feel like I am being deprived. I think planning your treats is key as you will be less likely to go hog wild. I hide these truffles in the deepest, darkest corner of my freezer. This is a necessary step to ensure my planned treats are there when I want and need them.

(My son has been known to dip into my special stash and devour the entire package in one gulp.) Food is one of the great pleasures in life, so definitely indulge in those special treats that bring you joy now and then.

## ELEVATING ACTIONS:

- Use the "kitchen is closed" mindset to keep you from rummaging the cupboards late at night to satisfy cravings.
- Brush and floss your teeth early in the evening to motivate yourself to keep your teeth clean and avoid late night snacks.
- Keep your vehicle stocked with a few healthy snacks in case of emergency.
- Plan for snacking so that you have healthy food on hand to fill you up with an extra boost when you need it.
- Fix yourself a nice comfort beverage next time you are feeling emotional and need a boost. You may find this just as soothing (if not more) than a piece of chocolate!
- Don't deprive yourself of your favorite treats. Plan for them and savour each bite!

# 7

# WEAR BLINDERS DOING HOUSEWORK

I think it is safe to say that most of us dream of a clean and tidy home, with all our belongings organized and in order. When my home is neat and orderly, I feel more light, serene and calm. I have always said, if given a choice, I would choose a clean house over a day at the spa every time! An uncluttered, peaceful environment leads to a tranquil state of mind.

In my fairy-tale dream world, I would wake up each morning to a sparkling, clean house with everything in its place. My perfect daydream home would make even Marie Kondo green with envy! Greeting such an ideal setting each morning would instantly elevate my mood and start my day off on the right foot.

The reality is, I live with three males, a dog and three parakeets. When we owned chickens, there were even times Rocky the rooster made an unwelcome appearance in the living room by strutting in an open door. Life in our household is bustling and messy and trying to maintain such high housekeeping standards would nearly kill me. (I know this because I have tried!) By the time I finished cleaning the house, it was time to start back at the beginning. I was running on a hamster wheel or housework!

I finally came up with a compromise that seems to fit the bill of "good enough". I choose to wear blinders when it suits, focusing my attention on certain priority areas and ignoring others (wearing blinders). This approach and attitude towards housework has lifted the weight off my shoulders and set me free of the desire for perfection. It has elevated the experience of enjoying my home instead of always focusing on the negative.

I categorized my house into priority vs non-priority zones. I like to start my day off feeling like the slate is clean. Descending the stairs to a messy kitchen in the morning is instantly deflating. I guess it makes me feel like I am already behind the eight ball and the day hasn't even started. My husband and I both agreed that the kitchen is the *number one* priority for the both of us. We really make it a team effort to ensure the kitchen is in an orderly state each evening with the counters wiped and the dishwasher turned on. It might not be perfect (remnants of late-night nacho making are often in the sink), but it is at least not a complete disaster zone.

The other area of our home we use and enjoy each morning is our living room. (This is not our TV room where the kids hang out. Walking into this room actually requires a blindfold!) Most mornings we enjoy our coffee/tea on the couch, chatting about our upcoming day and watching the birds at the feeder. Before heading to bed each night, I do a "quick and dirty" tidy of this area that involves picking up various dog toys strewn about the room, clearing stray items off the coffee table, and plumping the couch cushions. This room is fairly easy to keep in order, so the goal feels achievable. It is always a nice feeling to bask in the glow of success!

Blinders come in handy for all areas of the home my children use heavily. These include their bedrooms, the TV room and their bathroom. (We have our own ensuite.) Again, the fairy-tale version of my life would include robot children who are pre-programmed to make their beds upon waking and keep their rooms neat as a pin. It is safe to say my children are not robots (nor do I want them to be). I pick and choose my battles in life and spotless kids' rooms is not a fight I'm up for. Since, I rarely go in those rooms, other than to drop off laundry at the door, it is easy to ignore them. If I am really cranky at the sight of them, I just close the door! Out of sight, out of mind.

They have their own bathroom they are responsible for cleaning as part of their chores. Let's just say their cleaning standards are not the same as mine. The blinders go on here too. I have relinquished control, and as long as there is some level of effort going on with the chores, I am satisfied. There is some irony to the fact that lowering my standards has actually elevated my life.

I encourage you to take an inventory of your home and identify the key areas that are important to you when it comes to cleanliness and order. The kitchen is a great one to focus on because it is the hub of all activity in the house. Even if you just take on the kitchen, you will feel a great deal of satisfaction. Other areas that I suggest are ones that you have complete control over. These might include a home office or workspace that only you use. Your half of the closet might be another good choice. Even if your spouse's side is a disaster, you can have your clothing neatly and attractively displayed. I also chose my vanity. We have two sinks in the ensuite, so I keep my own personal space nice and tidy with my toiletries and makeup well-organized. I am the only one who uses this little space, so it is easy to keep it tidy and I enjoy having my personal care items attractively arranged.

## **ELEVATING ACTIONS:**

- Try to let go of the notion of a perfectly organized home and free yourself from the pressure of trying to maintain it.
- Prioritize key areas in your home where you would like to focus your cleaning and tidying efforts. Choose to ignore other areas that are less important.
- Make a list of tiny spaces that only you use. These could be added to your list of priorities since you are the only one using them and they will be easier to maintain.
- Accept or enlist help with household chores, but once you do so, relinquish control. You may have to lower your standards (a lot).

# 8

# ELEVATE YOUR LOOK IN THE REALM OF REALITY

Do you have a closet full of clothes that have never been touched, the price tags still intact? If you are nodding your head enthusiastically, then I can relate! I have been there. There are various reasons these brand-new garments may be left lonely and unworn. Maybe you have lost or gained weight. Maybe you bought the item on a whim and it matches nothing else you own. Or perhaps, it just doesn't suit your current lifestyle. Do you ever find yourself buying clothes for a life that exists only in your daydreams, but the opportunity to wear them never arises?

I am a huge fan of dressing nicely each day. I love putting effort into my appearance and dressing in a manner that makes me feel chic and pulled-together. It not only elevates my mood, but also makes me feel more productive! That being said, I am also a proponent of dressing for the reality of your lifestyle. It took me a long time to reconcile my desire to dress well with my messy, sometimes dirty life. For a number of years, I was a stay-at-home mom pulling on yoga pants and throwing her hair in a ponytail day after day. Nice clothes felt like a waste of time and money when I was spending my days changing diapers, finger painting and picking slugs out of the toy bin. (Kids collect strange things!)

Somewhere along the line, I changed my tune and my attitude. I noticed that when I put a bit more effort into my clothing and personal appearance, the world around me felt more elevated. Simply put, I felt better about myself and had a greater sense of dignity. It took me awhile, but I figured out a way to dress that suited my personal style, *and* fit nicely into my casual, rural lifestyle.

Early attempts to elevate my wardrobe sometimes resulted in failure. I would purchase something I really loved, but it would sit in the closet because it was too delicate for the activities of the day ahead. Other times I would go ahead and wear my new pretty garment, but I found myself avoiding tasks that might damage it. The concept of "using your best" really only works if there is not a 100% chance it will be ruined within minutes. In my house, the odds were stacked against me! As I mentioned, I faced a number of messy challenges that initially felt like road blocks in my quest to dress well:

- I drive a heavy-duty SUV and live on a rural property with a long, dusty gravel driveway. (When I pull into the garage, I am usually followed by a plume of dust that looks like a sandstorm on the Sahara.)
- For many years we owned chickens, ducks and sheep that needed daily tending. I currently have a dog that goes for daily walks in the woods.
- I have two active boys that enjoy activities such as skateboarding and mountain biking. Finding myself smeared in bicycle grease or mud is a common occurrence.
- Exercise is a big part of my life and is sprinkled throughout my day.
- We have a woodstove and burn four cords of firewood a year. Because I am the only one home all day, I look after the ferrying of the wood from the barn to the house on a daily basis.

Looking at this list, it was pretty clear that delicate dresses, white pants and high heels were simply not going to be practical choices for this country mouse.

What wardrobe road blocks are you up against in your life? Do you find yourself making excuses for not putting a little more effort into your appearance? Be honest with yourself and make a list of the problem areas you face. Are you also a stay-at-home mom, feeling burdened by the never-ending mess that seems to go hand-in-hand with small children? Do you commute to work by bicycle and feel like nicer clothes just aren't an option? Why not brainstorm for solutions to your problems and find creative ways to make your style goals a reality! I promise you, with a little effort and imagination, you can find a system that will suit you perfectly.

Taking care of your appearance, as shallow as it might sound, is very uplifting! Being realistic about your lifestyle and filling your closet with clothes you are not afraid to wear is certainly something to consider. I do have a small number of delicate wardrobe pieces for special events, but the bulk of my closet consists of stylish, but very wearable pieces.

Another factor to consider is the timing of activities during your day. Could you get through the messier jobs first thing? Could you bring a change of clothes (even just a top or bottom) if the walk to work leaves you sweaty? Would a chic, full-coverage apron solve most of your problems with sticky fingers and flying food particles?

I put a lot of thought into my own situation and came up with a dressing formula and a grooming schedule that works for me. Here are a few rules and tips I devised for myself that you might find useful:

- *Get the dirty work over with first!* As soon as I get up in the morning, I throw on my exercise clothes and do my workout. While still in my workout clothes, I tackle messier chores like sweeping the garage and bringing in a load of firewood.

- *Black and other dark colors are my best friends.* I need garments that just don't show the dirt, which is really inevitable. I am a dirt magnet.
- *Durable, washable fabrics are also my friends, especially on the bottom.* I can get away with a nice blouse or cashmere sweater, but jeans are still the best choice for me. I think they can look polished and a dark wash skinny really suits my figure. Jeans wash well, the fabric is sturdy, and they can be dressed up. In the summer I wear loose-fitting cotton or linen dresses that are easy to keep clean.
- *Rubber boots are one of my life essentials.* I take my little dog on a daily walk through the woods, which includes thorny branches and muddy paths. By this time of the day, I am fully dressed and groomed. I simply slip on a pair of tall rubber boots (my favorite style is the Aigletine by Aigle, made in France!) and a sturdy jacket, and I am on my way. The boots protect my jeans from mud and snags all the way up to my knees and the jacket protects my nice blouse or sweater underneath.
- *Don't be lazy and change your clothes if the situation calls for it.* If I am dressed in a nice blouse for the day and the boys beg me to take them to the skate park, I quickly change out of my top and slip on a black t-shirt. It only takes a minute and I usually have dark jeans on that can handle any messes. I will also switch

into a pair of cute casual sneakers if I am wearing delicate footwear.

- *There is no excuse for not taking the time to have a shower, do my hair, put on some light makeup and some pretty jewelry.* I always feel better about myself. I can still look cute and pulled together while I am piling firewood or hanging at the skate park. I once spent two months painting my entire house. My daily outfit consisted of a mechanic's suit, but I still put on my makeup, perfume and jewelry!

I am convinced that elevating your look (and in turn your mood) is possible for anyone! It might take a bit of creativity, and a bit of compromise, but it is achievable. Have some fun with it!

## **ELEVATING ACTIONS:**

- Take the time to put a bit of effort into your appearance each day. Even a small investment of time can have a big impact on your mood and productivity.
- Have a look at your current lifestyle and identify any roadblocks or challenges you face in dressing in a manner that would please you.
- Brainstorm solutions for your problem. Think about garments and fabrics that would best suit the reality of your situation.

- Consider the timing of the activities in your day and how that might impact your ability to dress the way you would like.
- Fill your wardrobe with wearable pieces that you love, but also suit your lifestyle.

# 9

# GET YOUR DAILY DOSE OF LEAFY GREENS

The title of this chapter implies that I am about to make a case for filling your plate with the likes of kale, spinach and swiss chard. While I am certainly a huge fan of these healthful foods and all the goodness they have to offer, I'd like to explore the other type of leafy greens that can elevate our lives.

As human beings, I believe that we are inherently drawn to interact with the natural world around us. In today's hectic and high-tech environment, it is often easy to become detached from nature. A number of years ago my husband sat beside a woman and her eight-year-old son on a business trip. A scene of a child running freely through a lush green field flashed on the in-flight video screen. The little boy turned to his mother and asked, "Mommy, isn't it dangerous to run through a field like that?" An hour later, while peering out the window, he asked his mother if the rural farm fields were golf courses.

Are today's children so "plugged into" technology and controlled, scheduled activities that they have completely lost touch with nature? It concerns me that the potential leaders of tomorrow may not have a hands-on appreciation for the natural world.

I read a book that touches on this very issue; *Last Child in the Woods: Saving Our Children from Nature Deficit Disorder* by Richard Louv. It is a must-read for every parent and really emphasizes the importance of providing our children with the opportunity to freely explore and discover the wonders of the natural world. Children need to get their hands dirty so to speak.

Of course, it's not just children that need a daily dose of nature! Personally, I have a strong physical and mental need to spend time outdoors each day, absorbing the energy from the abundance of life that surrounds me. I am a country girl, so the natural world has never been far from my doorstep. Growing up, I spent many hours exploring the fields, forests and hills surrounding our home. You could often find me perched high in a tree, engrossed in my favorite novel. (This is what lead to that broken arm that saved me from my dreadful piano lessons!)

Seeking out ways to spend time in nature each day does so much for the soul. Green is the dominant color in nature (at least for certain months of the year). The color green is said to evoke a sense of tranquility, abundance and renewal. Spending even a small amount of time surrounded by trees, flowers and all things green leaves me feeling refreshed and elevated.

Rain or shine, I usually make at least a small effort to get myself outside each day. With the proper outerwear, I can brave the messiest of weather for at least a small amount of time. My daily schedule includes a short walk in the woods with my dog. (He is a tiny toy poodle, so he doesn't need to go far!) On days this is not possible, I might spend a small amount of time just sitting on my deck, or dead-heading a few of my potted plants. I am not suggesting we all embark on a two-hour hike each day! Just soaking up some natural light and breathing fresh air for a short period of time can elevate your state of mind.

Could you make a commitment to yourself to try to incorporate at least a tiny bit of nature into your life each day? Maybe you also live in a rural setting and this is an easy challenge! Making a promise to yourself to actually get out there each day might be the push you need.

Perhaps you live in a city, and nature isn't at your doorstep. I used to live and work in a small city myself. Luckily, I lived in an apartment that was very close to a beautiful park. My husband and I would often venture into the park for an evening walk. It was so lovely to be immersed in the sounds of birds and squirrels under the canopy of ancient pine trees. Do you live or work close to a park or small green space? Could you take your packed lunch to a bench instead of chomping it down at your desk? Could you re-route your daily walk to work so that it takes you through a residential area with trees?

If you live in the city (or outside the city as well), you could centre your weekend plans around a nature outing. Perhaps a picnic in a local park or a day trip to a hiking location might be more enriching (and less expensive) than hitting the mall. Maybe your child plays soccer and the games are held outdoors. Instead of gossiping with the other parents, try taking a few moments to really notice your surroundings and appreciate the sun on your face. Make a point of taking in a few conscious breaths of fresh air. Being aware of the nature around you, instead of just going through the motions, really enhances the experience of being outdoors.

Even exercising your green thumb and tending to a few potted plants can be a rewarding way to connect with nature. I recently beautified my deck with an abundance of potted lavender plants. Even if it is raining, I can sit under the porch roof and listen to the raindrops while being immersed in the scent of lavender. It is very uplifting! I don't have a good track record with indoor house plants, but in the last couple of years I discovered succulents. They are pretty much indestructible and are a nice way to add a little greenery and nature to your home.

With all this talk of green, I almost forgot to mention winter. As a Canadian girl, there is no avoiding the cold weather. It is something I definitely struggle with. I have to push myself a lot harder to venture outside when the temperature drops. As I explained in chapter 5, I embarked on a personal mission to inspire myself to get outdoors more often by finding outwear that I love *and* that keeps me warm. I still run twelve months of the year. I don't enjoy my winter runs as much as the warm weather ones, but the time outdoors during those darkest of months really does boost my energy levels. I have some really good winter running gear that keeps me comfortable on most days. I can't say enough about dressing for the weather, particularly when it is cold!

## **ELEVATING ACTIONS:**

- Make a commitment to yourself to find a way (big or small) to spend time outdoors each day.
- Be creative with ideas for tapping into the natural world. Seek out ways to bring small moments into the fold of your day.
- When you are outdoors, be mindful of your surroundings. Instead of just travelling from point A to B, take the time to appreciate the sun, listen to the birds and breathe in the freshness.
- Try your hand at indoor gardening to bring a bit of greenery into your indoor space.
- Invest in proper outerwear that will allow you to enjoy the outdoors, rain or shine, snow or sleet!

# 10

# MAKE A DREAMY/ PRACTICAL LIST

There is a certain satisfaction that comes with physically crossing an item off my to-do list. In today's hectic world, it does not take long for our to-do lists to take on lives of their own, growing into uncontrollable beasts. Do you feel like you are facing each day with a list so long it feels unsurmountable? It can almost make you feel like giving up before you even get started! In order to save myself from "the beast", I've worked hard to tame it into something not only manageable, but enjoyable! Having a daily list that feels achievable *and* that is sprinkled with a little bit of magic can really elevate the tone of your day.

A number of years ago I started incorporating the concept of the dreamy/practical to-do list into my days. It was an idea I learned from a blogger named Mary Beth of www.saltandchocolate.blogspot.com. I have refined it over the years, but the basic concept remains the same.

Create to-do lists that incorporate both practical tasks (non-negotiable items that need to get done) and fun, dreamy activities. By including the dreamy items on your list, you are making a commitment to yourself that your day will be comprised of moments of peace and enjoyment. The act of writing these things down formalizes your commitment to nourishing your soul, instead of just putting out fires.

My daily to-do list certainly contains traditional uninspiring tasks such as gathering tax information and booking doctor appointments. It also includes taking my pup on his short walk in the woods, doing a ten-minute guided meditation on my phone, and perhaps gathering wildflowers to make a bouquet for the coffee table. Does it seem silly to write down picking flowers as a must-do item on my list? At first glance, it might, but this little action elevates both my mood and the atmosphere of our home. Reframed in this light, it takes on greater importance. The bottom line is, if you want your day to day life to include the dreamy along with the productive, you need to make time for these moments and prioritize them.

Even including just one dreamy item on your daily to-do list can have a significant impact. At the end of the day, it will give you the sense that you made time for yourself, even if it was only for a few minutes. Grab a journal and make a list of all the things you love to do, but never seem to find the time for. It is a good idea to categorize them by time commitment. Little tasks might include reading a chapter of the book on your night stand, arranging a bouquet you picked at the grocery store, taking a walk through the park on your lunch break, or enjoying a quiet cup of tea after dinner with a satisfying piece of dark chocolate. These are great little "happy hits" that you can incorporate into busy days with a little planning. Activities that involve a larger time commitment might best be saved for the weekend: Going on a nature hike, finally getting to that knitting project you have squirreled away, playing around with your paint set, refinishing an old dresser, leisurely browsing your favorite bookstore. Once you get started, I am sure it will not take you long to come up with an extensive list of items that qualify under the dreamy category!

The next step, of course, is to physically include the dreamy items in your daily planner (paper or electronic). I have found if I don't write them down and commit, the dreamier goals slip into the background of my mind as I become embroiled in the hustle and bustle of the day. Although I use technology to track many aspects of my life, I still rely on good old-fashioned pen and paper when working through daily to-do lists (again, I still enjoy the physical act of crossing items off). I searched high and low for a daily agenda that suited my needs, but eventually resorted to creating my own daily planning sheet as a Word document on my computer. I simply print off copies of my template and store the pages in a pretty three-ring binder. I was able to customize my agenda to include the various areas of my life I want to incorporate into each day. My list includes fitness activities, practical tasks, dreamy activities, appointments and my dinner menu for the day.

I recommend compiling your daily list of things to do with a conservative mindset. I keep the list minimal and realistic and usually only include practical tasks that really need to be dealt with. I keep an inventory of practical items on the side. If I discover I have extra time, I will pull an item off that list and mark it off as accomplished. By keeping my agenda manageable, I don't feel overwhelmed. It also means there is time for those important dreamy items! Nothing quite elevates me at the end of the day than having all the items on my list crossed off, especially the fun ones!

I enjoy starting my day with something that is just for me, which in most instances, is a morning run or workout video. I always make sure I wake up before the rest of the family to ensure I have time for this priority. Maybe you would enjoy kicking your day off with a set of stretches and an inspiring read. Beginning the day with something that lifts your spirits is so much more elevating than pushing the snooze button on repeat (which I did for many, many years)!

As the day rolls along, I like to use my dreamy to-do items as little rewards for completing less- inspiring tasks.

I like to cut deals with myself! One might be, "Once you finish updating the budget and finances, you can sit down with a cup of tea and read your favorite blog posts." When I worked in the city, I would often use my lunch break to do something relaxing like a walk on the waterfront or a lunch date with my husband. (We worked at the same office!) Instead of listening to the news on the commute home, why not pop on an audio book you've been dying to read but haven't found the time for. It is definitely nice to sprinkle a little bit of joy in your day and have those happy hits to look forward to. At the end of the day I often reward myself for cleaning up the kitchen with a nice hot bath. It motivates me to tackle the job so I can move on to something much more enjoyable.

## **ELEVATING ACTIONS:**

- Have fun compiling a list of dreamy activities you never find the time for. Separate them into quick little items and ones that require a larger time commitment.
- Commit to including at least one (hopefully more) of these items on your daily to-do list. Write it down!
- Keep your daily to-do list manageable. Always underestimate what you can accomplish in a day, so you don't feel overwhelmed. If you get more done than planned, you can celebrate!

- Why not start your day off with a dreamy activity to kickstart your mind, body and mood?
- Try using your dreamy to-do items as an incentive to get through the tougher tasks. Motivate yourself with them!

# 11

# SEEK OUT SKILLED BEAUTY ADVICE

Makeup was always a confusing and frustrating territory for me. I had a fair bit of acne growing up, so my main concern was always concealing my blemishes. My skin eventually cleared up, (ironically when I got pregnant at thirty) but at that point I was in a stage of life where I didn't pay much attention to my appearance on a daily basis. I was home full-time with two babies spaced a mere seventeen months apart and was struggling to even have a shower or get dressed each day.

Maybe my mother was trying to send me a subtle (or not so subtle) message, but she gave me Jennifer L. Scott's book *Lessons from Madame Chic* for my birthday. (Mothers are so great at finding sneaky ways to get their point across, aren't they?) Reading this book was a turning point for me. Jennifer opened my eyes to the possibility that dressing presentably and freshening up my face with a "no-makeup look" might make me feel better about myself. Putting some time and effort into your appearance sounds superficial. Obviously, what's going on inside is much more important than outside! That being said, I have experienced first-hand how transformative and elevating a bit of time in front of your vanity mirror can have on your self-confidence.

We all have different skill levels in the beauty department. Mine were non-existent and so was my inventory of cosmetics. I owned three items; concealer, blush and lip gloss (and one blush brush). I have a childhood friend who always had the most perfect, clear and creamy complexion on earth. I ran into her recently, and she still maintains this beautiful glow in her mid-forties. She doesn't wear a lick of makeup, and she looks amazing! Honestly, I don't think anyone *needs* makeup, but it can give your face a fresh boost if that is what you are looking for.

Looking in the mirror, I felt a *fresh boost* was certainly required. Those days of sun-worshiping as a teen hadn't done me any favours. New little brown spots were making daily appearances. They matched the dark circles under my eyes from years of sleep deprivation. I was convinced a little makeup was in order, but I had no idea where to start!

As I have established, I am no beauty guru and I would be the last person you would want to take advice from at the makeup counter. I am not color blind, but it often feels as though I am when faced with the infinite number of products and color choices available these days. I freeze. I can't seem to distinguish warm from cool or pink from peach! There was a lot of trial and error (and money wasted) in the beginning of my makeup journey.

After plenty of tinkering on my own, with the odd piece of advice from a sales clerk, I made a decision to book an appointment at my favorite spa for a makeup lesson. This was money well-spent and I highly recommend the experience. YouTube videos and beauty counter advice are great, but considering my lack of knowledge in this area, the lesson was the way to go. I specifically requested an aesthetician I knew well and whose own makeup application I really admired. I felt confident that her "style" was similar to the look I was going for. I knew with certainty she wouldn't lead me down the wrong path. I wanted a very simple, easy day-time look that used minimal products. She was so lovely and never pressured me to buy any of the spa's products. I brought all my own makeup and brushes and we used as much of these items as possible. I ended up going home with a new set of eyeshadow and a whole lot more confidence in my abilities! My morning makeup routine takes about ten minutes and gives both my face and my mood a boost each day.

Maybe you are already a master of makeup and beauty products and have this area of your life well covered. (Maybe you should be the one offering lessons!) Perhaps you enjoy experimenting with makeup, but your beauty routine feels stale and could use a little upgrade. As we enter different seasons of life (aka aging), the colors and application techniques best suited to our features may change over time. A makeup lesson is a great way to refresh and modernize your look. I am actually contemplating booking another session now that I am more comfortable with makeup application, as I know there are many tricks and tips still to learn. There are most likely stores, or even spas, that offer lessons for free. Perhaps you have a friend who is a marvel with makeup who would absolutely love to help you out (fun girls' night idea)!

As we all know, YouTube has unlimited makeup and beauty product tutorials right at our fingertips. I think this serves as a great resource for someone who already has basic skills and might be looking to do a bit of tweaking. Perhaps you want to learn how to do a dramatic smoky eye or perfect your under-eye coverage. I personally found the number of videos overwhelming as a starting point. I also wasn't interested in complex techniques such as contouring, and I had difficulty sifting through all the options.

Sales clerks at the counters can also offer great advice, although my experience is that the level of service you receive is often hit or miss. Sometimes I do not trust their advice because I feel they are under pressure to up-sell. Do I really need that specialized brush just to apply my under-eye concealer? Aren't my own fingertips good enough?

Whatever your skill set, revisiting and revamping your makeup routine is a fun and elevating way to spice up your life a little.

## **ELEVATING ACTIONS:**

- Give your current makeup routine some consideration and ask yourself if it might be time for an upgrade or renewal.
- Consider booking a personal makeup lesson so you can benefit from expert advice and color choices tailored just for you.
- Do you have a friend with fantastic makeup skills and style? Ask her for assistance! She will likely feel very flattered and happy to help you out.
- Have fun exploring new ideas and tricks on YouTube.
- If you are a makeup guru, why not offer to help a friend in need!

# 12

# SCRUB THE POTTY MOUTH

Have you recently parked outside a middle school at dismissal time? The first time I waited outside my son's grade six school, my jaw literally dropped. Call me naïve, but I had no idea cursing and swearing had become so widely *accepted* in our society. I guess it wasn't the sound of twelve-year-olds dropping f-bombs that shocked me, but the fact they were doing it freely in the presence of teachers and the principal. No one batted an eye. I felt a bit sad in that moment, realizing the sweet and innocent days of my little boys were slipping away. When I expressed my surprise at the use of this language in front of the teachers, my son just matter-of-factly stated, "Oh yeah, that's just normal." Sigh!

I didn't grow up in a household where there was a lot of cursing. My father spat out a few offensive terms now and then when his temper got the best of him. Yes, even my sweet, poised and polite mother might be caught uttering a minorly offensive term under her breath when she thinks no one can hear her. I definitely did my fair share of swearing as a teenager. In my adolescent quest to be cool and fit in, I followed the pack on a number of occasions. Back then we at least kept out potty mouths shut in fronts of the adults and maintained some level of respect for their authority. We had a sense of an invisible line that was not to be crossed. We let loose with our friends, but knew when to reel it in.

My foul language continued into adulthood; I am ashamed to admit. Articling as an accounting student, the firm's social environment was essentially an extension of university. The office had a very young, social vibe that included a lot of partying with co-workers. What I have found is the more time you spend around people who use foul language, the easier it is to fall back into old habits.

Not surprisingly, when I had my first child at the age of thirty and became a stay-at-home mother, the swearing just stopped. It felt easy and natural to shut it off. Instead of spending my days joking with co-workers, I was tending to my sweet innocent baby. *Of course* I was going to be careful with my words. It really took no thought or effort. The habit was broken.

I am not living in a dream world. My husband argues that it is more accepted now, and as a result, many of these terms are considered less offensive. He also works as an accountant, and things have only gotten worse in the business world since my days at the office. I am of the opinion that I don't care what everyone else is doing. I try not to use the actions of others to justify my own. My personal goal is to stop swearing altogether (knowing full-well I will likely never achieve perfection). There is a time and place for the odd curse word, but as far as most of my day to day interactions, it doesn't really suit the person I am striving to be.

Being mindful with your words not only elevates your state of mind, it elevates the image you portray to others. It elevates conversations! I have reminded my children that the language they use portrays an image to the world. How would a teacher feel about writing a glowing reference letter for someone who can't form a complete sentence without three obscenities included?

Again, I am being realistic, and will be the first to admit there are certain times in life where cursing just *feels good*. And yes, sometimes it is funny. The language in many of today's comedies is over the top. I actually think swearing could have a greater comedic effect if used more selectively. Have you ever seen the classic John Candy/Steve Martin film *Planes, Trains and Automobiles*? Steve Martin's character faces so many irritating and temper inducing situations throughout the film. Interestingly, there is very little cursing, if any. He finally *loses it* in the car rental scene and the selective use of the f-bomb in this case actually enhances the scene, if I dare say. If he had been cursing constantly throughout the film, (like the middle schoolers) this specific scene would not have been as funny or effective in communicating his sense of desperation.

Maybe you cleaned up your potty mouth long ago. Maybe you never had one to begin with. (If so, I applaud you!) Maybe your clean-up efforts are still a work-in-progress. It might not be as easy to change old habits as just simply declaring you will stop. Certain words do travel quickly to the tip of the tongue in moments of anger or frustration. I do, however, think that setting an intention to be mindful of your language is a great place to start.

Since writing this chapter, I have noticed it is more top of mind for me. I have a tendency to slip up when I am chatting alone with my husband (yes, he can be a bit of a bad influence)! If I keep my goals top of mind, it is easier to catch myself and perhaps replace the offensive word with a less offensive one. Maybe you can think of a few new "go to" words. I'm guessing many of us have developed strong neuro-pathways that lead us to automatically reach for certain words in heated moments. Could you re-wire yourself with a less offensive word like the classic fudge or sugar? I actually think it might be fun to think of new fresh and modern replacement words. Be creative! It could provide some comic relief.

Perhaps an easy way to clean up your language might be to focus on the big important words first (e.g. the f-bomb). Save the more minor, less offensive terms for another day. You might find that by starting small and taking that first step, you naturally omit the other words from your vocabulary as well.

Lastly, elevating the content of what you are exposed to is another great approach. Cursing has become normalized in our society, so the more we hear it, the easier it is to incorporate it into our lives. I can't do anything about the school yard, but we do try hard to watch films that at least *limit* the foul language. I have two teens, so our family is definitely past the Disney phase. It can be challenging to find entertainment for this age group that is not riddled with obscenities. Our family isn't perfect, but we do try to incorporate the concept of "elevate" when choosing entertainment options.

## **ELEVATING ACTIONS:**

- If you have a tendency to use a lot of foul language, try setting an intention to improve in this area. Remind yourself of your goal regularly throughout the day.
- Try replacing "old favorites" with new, less offensive substitutions.

- Start small if you need to. Pick the *one word* you want to delete from your vocabulary and focus your attention solely on it.
- Limit your exposure to foul language as much as possible by choosing "cleaner" films, music and reading material more often.

# 13

# THINK OUTSIDE THE BIG BOX WHEN SHOPPING

My husband and I started collecting furniture for our home long before the plans were even drawn up. I had been a lover of "all things old" since childhood, so it was natural that I chose to furnish my home, for the most part, with antiques. We have a casual farmhouse-style house, so we were not looking for expensive or rare items. We discovered that we were able to furnish our house in unique, high quality pieces, while still spending less than you would at a furniture store. A simple pine dresser beaming with rustic charm and patina costs about the same as something made of pressboard from Ikea! We even purchased old barn boards for our flooring. The product was cheaper than new wide-plank flooring and possesses much more character.

The experience of home building and furnishing helped me think outside the box when looking to build a wardrobe. In my early thirties, I found myself in a bit of a style "crisis". I was a stay-at-home mom with two busy toddlers underfoot, barely able to find the time or energy to change out of my pajamas each day. When I finally decided to up my game and start putting more effort (and money) into my appearance, I was pretty much starting from scratch. I was not one of those people with an overflowing closet. My closet consisted of a few t-shirts and jeans and one pair of leather shoes. (I'm not exaggerating about the shoes!) Any clothing leftover from my corporate career was maternity wear stuffed in storage. I'm not going to get into my style transformation here (that might just be an entire book on its own), but needless to say I needed to invest in some clothing!

Perhaps it is human nature to be drawn to "pretty things". When I walk into a store, I am magnetically drawn to those items with the higher price tags. It doesn't matter what it is! It could be a new bathroom tile, or a beautiful sweater. I definitely have an affinity for quality materials (which often goes hand in hand with a higher price tag).

With my clothing budget in hand, I set out to build a new wardrobe from the ground up. To my dismay, I soon discovered there was a disconnect between my style goals and my budget. Many of the higher quality items I was attracted to were pricey! I'm not talking luxury brands, but rather brands that trended toward higher prices. The Citizens of Humanity jeans I discovered fit my body *perfectly* and lifted my butt *just so*, were two hundred dollars. I have no doubt there are many great jeans out there with much lower price tags, but I had fallen in love with t*hese*.

My approach to shopping for clothing varies based on the article I am looking for. I have developed some strategies for seeking out deals on some of the pricier items on my wish list. Shopping on the second-hand market provides the opportunity to elevate your wardrobe without paying full price for higher-end items. By shopping in consignment stores and on sites such as eBay and The RealReal, I have been able to include items in my wardrobe that I would never dream of paying full price for. I will admit, buying brand new is a lot simpler. Walking into a boutique or clicking an item into an electronic basket can be much easier and less time consuming than exploring the used market. I certainly buy new often. I don't shop second-hand exclusively, but rather incorporate this method into my arsenal of shopping strategies.

Shopping the second-hand market can be overwhelming if you don't know where to start. I first experimented with this approach by visiting my local high-end consignment shops. Please don't envision digging through mountains of used clothing in bins. Though I have heard stories of treasures found at this type of shop, I do not have the time or energy for this approach. These shops are set up like a regular boutique, with clothing very nicely displayed and organized. Prices are typically 25-40% of the original retail price.

My first suggestion when shopping at consignment stores is to arm yourself with a list. It is just as easy to impulse buy in this setting as anywhere. In fact, it may be easier, because you will find yourself justifying a purchase with the phrase, "It's such a good deal". I use an app called WishList to track items I am hunting for. It might be a wool navy coat or a silk blouse by Equipment. This keeps me on track when I am browsing so I feel focused.

Consignment shops are constantly receiving new stock, so it is best to check in frequently. Most of them have social media accounts where they post regularly. This is a great way to keep an eye out for an item on your wish list without making a trip into the store. Often you can request that the shop keep track of a particular item on your shopping list for you. When that gorgeous pair of Frye riding boots finally arrives in your size, they are often happy to give you first dibs before putting it on the floor. Next time you are planning a purchase, why not check out your local consignment shop first? You may be pleasantly surprised!

Shopping at consignment stores can involve a time commitment, and it certainly can take a while for that perfect item you have been looking for to appear.

Another route is to shop online, which can be a daunting task if you don't know where to start. There are a number of sites that specialize in brand name second-hand clothing such as The RealReal and Vestiaire Collective. Your location really dictates whether these are good avenues to try. I live in Canada, so both of these sites can be very cost prohibitive for me with high shipping and duty rates.

Accessories such as handbags, scarves and jewelry are an easy place to start because you do not need to be concerned with fit. Etsy is a wonderful venue to find estate jewelry at a decent price. I was looking to upgrade my jewelry collection with some classic gold hoop earrings. I picked up a couple of pairs of solid gold hoops on Etsy and was really pleased with them. I make sure I always read the shop reviews and examine the photos carefully, and I have yet to be burned.

When it comes to footwear or articles of clothing, I suggest starting with an item that you already know you love and will fit you. Maybe you saw a brand name cashmere sweater at the department store but baulked at the price. You already know your size, so buying it on eBay is likely very low risk. Perhaps you already own a pair of Paige jeans in a denim blue but are looking for the same style in black. These are low risk purchases. I usually only choose items that are new with tags (NWT) or new without tags (NWOT) because it is very difficult to assess the level of wear from photographs.

I have discovered that an item you are coveting will eventually pop up if you are willing to wait long enough. I have automatic searches set up on a few websites for pieces on my wish list. I receive an alert if one of these items has been recently listed. I was looking for a Smythe surplus jacket I had seen on Rachel McAdams. It is a military-style wool coat in army green that is actually from the brand's 2009 collection. I eventually was able to find it on eBay in my size for $100. This jacket probably retailed at $600. It is unique, edgy, classic and timeless and I *love* it (and apparently so does my twin Rachel). It's one of those pieces that instantly elevates my look, and it never would have been mine if I hadn't found it at such a great deal. Patience pays off!

I encourage you to think outside the box with your shopping and give second-hand a try. Make it a fun adventure and see yourself as embarking on a treasure hunt. When you finally find that perfect item, you might just appreciate it more!

## **ELEVATING ACTIONS:**

- Explore the world of second-hand shopping as a tool to elevate your wardrobe with higher-end and higher-quality pieces that might normally be out of your price range.
- Maintain a wish list of items you are searching for, so you approach shopping in an organized, well-

thought out manner. This decreases impulse buying (and regret).
- Check out your local consignment stores and follow them on social media. Make the shop staff aware of a special item you are searching for and ask them to notify you if it appears.
- To lower the risk of bad purchases, stick with items you know and love that you feel confident will fit you well.
- Accessories are a great place to dip your toe into the second-hand market as fit is less of a concern.
- Have patience! Know that eventually, that item you are coveting will appear and it will be worth the wait!
- Have fun with the process and approach it with the mindset that you are treasure hunting.

# 14

# ELEVATE MORE THAN JUST BODY PARTS WITH EXERCISE

If I could offer *just one* piece of advice on how to elevate the experience of your daily life, it would be to include some form of exercise into your day. Hands down, this single act has had the greatest impact on my life; lifting and improving my mood, sleep, mindset, waistline, energy levels and overall fitness. It doesn't matter if you have your makeup perfectly applied and your scarf tied just so, if you have lack-lustre energy, it will be a challenge to make it through the day feeling elevated, inspired and productive. Regular physical activity provides a boost of vitality that can then permeate all areas of your life.

I realize this comes easier to some of us than others. I am passionate about physical fitness, but this wasn't always the case. I was active as a child, but I was not exactly an athlete. I tinkered around with a few sports in high school, but I was never very committed or particularly talented at them. During my university years, my diet of pizza, instant noodles and breakfast cereal did nothing for my waistline or my energy levels. Walking to and from class was the extent of my daily fitness efforts (note that I lived in an apartment across the street from the lecture hall). I am now in my mid-forties, and physical activity is an integral part of my life. Of all the life improvements I have made over the years, adding exercise was actually the first. Adopting this one positive habit then had a snowball effect, as I picked up other health-promoting behaviours over time. Again, it has had the most significant impact, and that is probably why I have been able to stick with my daily routine for over twenty years. Feeling good is addictive!

There are no shortcuts or magic potions when it comes to improving your level of physical fitness. You have to put in the time and effort if you want results, and only *you* can do this. I believe no matter what circumstance you find yourself in, if you *want* it, you can make it happen. The key word is *want*. The question you must ask yourself is, "How badly do I want it?" If you feel strongly enough about improving your level of fitness, then it becomes a priority in your life, and you find a way to make it happen. I suspect those who complain that they can't find the time, or they don't like exercise just do not *want* the results enough. If you desire a trimmer tummy, a stronger heart and a boost to your energy level, you have the power to make it happen. Isn't that wonderful news to hear? It's all under your control and the results are up to you. It is actually empowering to frame it in this light. You have the power!

Find something you love to do and that makes your heart sing! I often hear people lamenting that they hate exercise. In fact, back in my early twenties I said the same thing! Maybe it is not exercise that they hate, but the feeling of being out of shape and out of breath. The solution is to get out and move the body! Certainly, there is a bit of a hurdle to jump at the start, but once that line is crossed, the benefits start pouring in. You will find yourself hooked on feeling energized and healthy.

I personally prefer activities to sports because they are more convenient and easier to incorporate into a daily routine. Walking, hiking, running and cycling are all easy to do anytime, anywhere. You do not need to drive to a class or rely on a partner or teammate to complete your workout. Perhaps mixing up your schedule would be a good approach if you are someone who likes working out in the company of others. My husband plays pick-up hockey three days a week, but also cycles and surfs. He enjoys the competition and comradery that hockey provides. That being said, he finds cycling and surfing to be more flexible as they are activities he can do independently and to suit his schedule. There are so many choices out there from dance classes, to online fitness programs, to a simple daily walk down your street!

This abundant buffet of options offers something for everyone, at any age. Challenge yourself with a new activity or re-discover something you loved in the past. If you are having fun while doing it, it will not feel like a chore, but rather a blessing in your life. Your inner voice will be saying, "Yay! I get to work out." Instead of, "Darn, I have to work out".

Another excuse I often hear is, "I don't have the time". As I mentioned before, you are in control! If you make physical activity a priority in your life, you can always make room for it. If you are scrolling your phone or reading the news for twenty minutes a day, you have time to exercise. I have done many fitness programs that call for workouts lasting a mere twenty minutes a day. The results I achieved from these programs were actually quite shocking, considering the small time commitment required each day. Could you set your alarm thirty minutes earlier each day? The morning is a wonderful time to include such an energy-boosting activity into your day. Maybe you can take a walk during your lunch break instead of mindlessly eating your sandwich at your desk. I encourage you to reflect on how you are spending your time each day. Could any of those mindless moments be put to better use?

Be sure to add your fitness activity to you daily to-do list. Writing it down will make it feel like it is a formal commitment to yourself and just as important (if not more) than anything else on the agenda for the day.

I have had many ups and downs over the last twenty years, but exercise has been a constant. When I was pregnant, I tapered down my running and walked each day instead. I was in a minor car accident a few years ago, which really set me back. I found small ways to move my body each day, even if it was just a walk around my yard. Last year I suffered a terrible case of tennis elbow which completely restricted all my upper body efforts. I just carried on with walking and running and set the weights aside for a while. There is usually *something* you can do to stay active. Staying flexible and ridding yourself of the "all or nothing mindset" will keep you on track, even when faced with life's many challenges.

The key to reaping the benefits of physical activity over the long run is consistency. We all get inspired and powered up when we start a new activity or routine. We need to realize that a lifetime of fitness is a marathon and not a sprint. My father is eighty-two years old and still cycles, hikes and attends the gym regularly. I am a strong believer that the key to his longevity and vitality is his consistent effort, year over year.

When it comes to exercise, the more you give, the more you get. It is human nature to seek the path of least resistance. If you want to improve your level of fitness and gain strength, you do need to push yourself a little outside the comfort zone. Maybe it's time to try putting a little more pep in your step on that morning walk! Playing some inspiring fast-paced music might be the boost you need to get yourself motivated. If you are lifting weights, is it time to bump up to something a little heavier? Challenging yourself in a safe way builds strength, self-confidence and results!

## **ELEVATING ACTIONS:**

- You have the power to make fitness a priority in your life. Make the decision today to include regular physical activity in your daily routine.
- Find an activity that you love to do! Challenge yourself with something new or re-visit an old passion from years gone by.
- Take an objective look at your day and decide on the best time to schedule in your daily dose of physical activity. Write it down and make the commitment to yourself to stick to your goals.
- Consistency is the key to long term benefits. When you face one of life's many roadblocks, get creative! Change up your routine or activities so that they fit with your current situation. Drop the all-or-nothing mindset.
- Give yourself a little nudge now and then to push a little harder. Relish and celebrate the increase in strength and improvement in results. You will be rewarded by your increased efforts!

# 15

# SELF SOOTHE IN AN UPLIFTING MANNER

None of us are immune to the ups and downs of life. There are, of course, the *big* stressful events or situations that completely knock us off our feet. Survival mode is often the only way to get through these times. All of us also face day to day stressors and anxieties that can drag us down and lead us to seek escape or comfort at the end of the day. In our quest for self-soothing, we all use different tactics and techniques to comfort or distract ourselves from the trials and tribulations of life. Some of these practices, are healthier than others!

I am not encouraging anyone to hide their head in the sand when it comes to dealing with personal issues. That being said, I think it is beneficial to find ways to self soothe and relax at the end of a hectic day (or during the day of course). It is unfortunate that the comforts many of us instinctively reach for can often leave us feeling worse than we did in the first place. Instead of elevating our experience they can push us further away from our goals in life. Yes, I'm talking about you wine and chocolate!

I wasn't sure if what I was observing was a new trend, or just a reflection of the fact I am currently categorized as middle-aged, but over the last ten years I have noticed more talk and chatter about drinking among women. The memes out there promoting, encouraging and normalizing the "mommy wine culture" are endless. A quick google search of drinking rates among women (in particular those classified as middle-aged) reveals that they are steadily on the rise. More often than ever before, women are turning to alcohol to deal with the effects of the stress in their lives.

I stopped drinking in my early twenties and never looked back. My last morning hung-over on the bathroom floor, still wearing the party dress, was the straw that broke the camel's back. The scene was getting old and I had reached a breaking point. With a small frame and a finicky gut, alcohol never sat well in my system. One drink left me feeling loopy, and the morning after always resulted in an unsettled stomach. It came down to two things. I was out of university and working my first full-time job that called for long hours. I had limited free-time and weekends quickly became sacred. I didn't want to waste my precious days off sleeping in and not being able to take advantage of the day. Secondly, I just liked "me" better completely sober. I liked the real version of myself better than the buzzed one. I really only drank for five years of my life, and during that time my relationship with alcohol was not a healthy one.

I started drinking in university as a way to fit in with the cool kids. It is easy to shake my head in dismay at this fact now, but this is pretty standard teen and young adult behaviour. I went to a small-town university with a big party atmosphere. Drinking was a huge part of the social scene. The party scene and the student atmosphere carried on while articling at the accounting firm.

Even very small amounts of alcohol bother my system. Once I quit there was no going back. I never saw any point in having the odd glass of wine here and there. Alcohol is just not something that adds to my life, so it is best to just exclude in completely.

Although I personally don't drink, I am not here to promote an anti-alcohol stance or look down upon those who choose to consume it. I am not trying to come across as judgemental. I completely understand that for many, alcoholic beverages provide a great deal of enjoyment and often enhance the experience of a meal. I do, however, think it is a worthwhile experience for all of us to examine the habits we use to comfort ourselves and relax. An honest answer to the question, "Is this helpful or hurtful?" might surprise you and allow you to re-think some of your behaviours. A small amount of wine with a special Friday night dinner sounds just fine. Often, however, the first glass is poured in the kitchen while chopping vegetables. One glass easily turns into two or three (or the whole bottle). Maybe "the weekend" is now starting early for you, with drinks on Thursday night instead of waiting until Friday. Perhaps you just *can't* unwind at the end of the day without that *one* (or more) glass of vodka to numb out the worries in your head.

Only you can determine what is right for you when it comes to alcohol consumption. Are your drinking habits keeping you from reaching any goals in life? Are the extra calories holding your back from attaining your weight loss objectives? Is the numbing effect preventing you from facing certain issues?

Both my parents, who I would definitely classify as Francophiles, used to enjoy wine quite frequently. In fact, they live two doors down from a winery and even participate in the autumn grape harvest! That being said, they have really cut back on their wine consumption in recent years (to the point of nearly eliminating it), finding the odd glass at a special celebration more than enough to suit them. Wine each evening with dinner just didn't feel right for them anymore.

Unhealthy "comfort" food is the other easy one to reach for during times of stress. The problem, of course, is that the pleasure received from that slice of chocolate cake lasts merely minutes (or seconds)! Once it is gone, you are left with the same empty feeling you were trying to fill, only now you likely feel worse. Bloated and guilty, you might find yourself reaching for a second slice to numb out the feelings again. It can be a vicious circle! Of course, we all enjoy treat foods and they certainly do add to the enjoyment of our lives! Once again, it is helpful to step back and look at your behaviours objectively. Are you using food in a nourishing, joyful manner (helpful) or as a tool to distract and numb yourself from your anxieties and negative feelings (hurtful)?

There are so many great options for self-soothing that can actually be beneficial to your mind and body. It is a helpful exercise to put pen to paper and actually make a list of all the soothing strategies you would like to keep in your toolkit. When you are feeling low, and headed for the carton of ice cream, pull out your list! It is nice to have an inventory of options on hand. During low moments, our mind is often not open to options other than those we are craving. I thought it would be fun to share my own list with you. These offer a great starting point and you can add and delete as it suits you.

- Have a warm, relaxing bath with your favorite and most luxurious bath products.
- Spend ten minutes doing some stretching.
- Make yourself a warm drink that will comfort and soothe you without packing in the calories.
- Take a delicious nap.

- Snuggle up with a pet.
- Give yourself a boost of energy with rigorous exercise. The physical burn might distract you from your worries.
- Instead of girls' night with drinks, try a girls' walk and chat around the neighbourhood.
- Lose yourself in a steamy, scandalous bubble gum book!
- Lose yourself in high-quality literature.
- Fill a basin with warm soapy water and soak your feet while you watch TV.
- Put on a movie and just lose yourself in the story line *without* losing yourself in a bag of chips.
- Pick one teeny tiny area in your home and do a quick, energizing tidy session.
- Lie back, close your eyes and listen to some relaxing music. No movement necessary.
- Lie back, close your eyes and lose yourself in an audiobook.
- Do a short or long guided meditation (there are so many on various apps and YouTube!)
- Call or text a friend or loved one who has a knack for lifting your mood.
- Watch funny comedy skits on YouTube.
- Keep a pitcher of water with cucumber slices in the fridge. Reach for your "spa water" when you feel the urge for a drink.
- Work on a craft project you can lose yourself in like knitting.

- Put your feet up and peruse old family photo albums.
- Scroll through the photos on your phone and enjoy the fun memories they provide.

As evidenced by this list, there are *so many* healthy, fun, energizing, relaxing and soothing options we can turn to when we are feeling sad, anxious or deflated. Reach for those that will elevate you instead of those that will drag you further down than you already are.

## **ELEVATING ACTIONS:**

- Take an honest look at the activities you turn to in times of stress or anxiety. Give yourself a sincere answer to the question, "Are these actions helping me or hurting me?"
- Brainstorm a list of all the different options available for times you are feeling low. Be creative and have fun with the list.
- Next time you find yourself needing a bit of comfort, pull out your list and try your new ideas. Make note of how these new self-soothing actions make you feel compared to past less helpful behaviours.

# 16

# ACQUIRE INTIMATES THAT INSPIRE

Your intimates and sleepwear are the first and final articles of clothing that grace your body each day. They can really set the tone for how you feel about your figure. Imagine the contrasting images of these two scenarios and the atmosphere and mindset they breed.

You jump out of the shower and reach blindly into the messy disarray of your underwear drawer. With little thought or consideration, you pull out the first pair of panties on hand. Ah, it's those good old faithful ones again. (Actually, that's all that is in there, so it is no surprise!) Boring, bland, utilitarian, nude in color, extremely comfortable (old faithfuls usually are), and oh so uninspiring. You slip them on with little thought and reach for a bra. You already find yourself anticipating the relief of removing this dreaded uncomfortable piece at the end of the day. It will have to do. You are in a rush and there is no time to rummage through the laundry bin for your favorite (which has been sitting there for two weeks). Off you go to get dressed with these two ghastly pieces as the foundation of your outfit and mood for the day.

Now let us dream up a much more pleasant and uplifting start to your day! You hop out of your luxurious morning shower and sense a tickle of excitement as you approach your underwear drawer. Your beautifully arranged drawer of pretty, lacy undies almost looks like a thoughtful display at a boutique. It uplifts your spirit in that moment just to admire it. You carefully select a matching bra and panty set that makes you feel sexy and feminine. They feel incredibly comfortable and sumptuous on your freshly washed and moisturized skin. You took the time last year to visit a boutique and have a proper bra fitting. What a world of difference it has made to own a bra that finally fits! Before completing your dressing, you take a moment to admire yourself in the mirror, appreciating your beautifully imperfect feminine body. Yes, you are just facing another day at the office and running the kids to soccer practice, but somehow just knowing that you are dressed well from the inside out elevates your mood and mindset. You walk a little taller, your pretty underpinnings your own personal little secret.

Which scenario sounds like your current situation? I lived in scenario number one for most of my adult life. My "underpinnings" consisted mainly of sports bras (which have their place in life), and plain black underwear purchased in "bulk" on sale at the department store. I gave little thought to my underwear. I think it was my way of avoiding issues and frustrations I had with my body image. Statistically speaking, my bosom size (or lack thereof) sits on the far-reaching outskirts of the bell curve. I have spent my whole life trying to find something to fit my flat chest. (I stuffed my prom and wedding dresses with shoulder pads!) Sure, I had read all the "how to dress like a French woman" advice on sexy lingerie. My issue was that my bra size was not sold in stores! At the age of forty-four, I finally took accurate measurements and came in at 30AAA. (I had no idea this size actually existed either.)

I will thank the universe that I live in the age of on-line shopping. A quick Google search and it turned out that there were others just like me out there! I discovered a sweet, lovely designer who specializes in "petite" bras sizes (www.elmashop.co). I sent her my measurements and she created the most amazing little silk and lace bras that fit me *perfectly*. The price I paid for them appeared steep at first glance, but factoring in all the ill-fitting bras that have ended up in the garbage, they were indeed a good investment. With the risk of sounding overly dramatic, finally finding a proper-fitting bra was a life changing experience for me. I upgraded my bottoms in the process too, and I now have an undies drawer that makes my heart sing.

The interesting thing is that after so many years of insecurity, I was finally able to appreciate and love my "petite" chest. The simple act of dressing it beautifully allowed me to change my mindset and appreciate the positive aspects of my body.

Maybe you are on the other end of the spectrum, or somewhere in between. I suggest having a proper bra fitting and finding a few that are not only comfortable, but pretty and inspiring. The same goes for your knickers. Putting something close to your body that is feminine and beautiful might just uplift your body image like it did for me. You don't have to spend a ton of money on the finest lingerie. I had custom bras made out of necessity, but not all my panties are expensive. (They are pretty though!)

Perhaps you upgraded your underwear drawer long ago! If so, it is always a refreshing and uplifting experience to take a few moments to dump out the contents and do a little organizing and rearranging. I like to add this to my to-do list when I change my closet over each season. Do you have a few items hanging around that are well past their prime that need to be tossed?

While your undies might be the first piece of clothing you reach for each day, your sleep and loungewear caps off your day and sets the tone for your evening. Because I wake so early in the morning (usually at 5 a.m.), I retire early as well. If we have nothing on in the evening, I like to put on my pajamas after dinner so I can relax and unwind in comfort.

I enjoy feeling elegant and pulled together, even in my loungewear, so I have invested in a few items that suit my needs. I have a very minimal sleepwear collection that I simply wash often. My small selection of items adds a pleasant vibe to the time I spend relaxing and sleeping. I have a few main criteria when choosing sleepwear. Since I have two teen boys in the house, I need something I feel comfortable wearing in front of them. I also take the dog out in the mornings, so I need to feel decent walking around our yard. Most importantly, I enjoy items that are pretty and attractive and keep me from looking like I am on my way to a slumber party. In the winter I wear two-piece menswear inspired PJ's. I picked up a really nice pair of silk Equipment pajamas on eBay that have lasted me for years. During the warmer months, I go for the same look, but in shorts. I have a silk shorts and tank set, and a bamboo shorts and shirt set. They work for my lifestyle at the moment and add a bit of sparkle to my downtime. I do have a few nighties that I wear infrequently since they don't fit the "wear around my children" item on the checklist!

Sleepwear is often an area of the wardrobe that is ignored or falls to the bottom of the priority list on the clothing budget. I will admit, I would probably choose a new blouse over a new set of PJ's. This might be an area that you need to pick away at over time. Pajamas are often a typical holiday gift item, so if people in your life are asking for ideas, why not drop a few hints for some beautiful PJ's? This might be a perfect opportunity to elevate your loungewear!

## **ELEVATING ACTIONS**

- Clean out your underwear drawer and assess the condition and beauty of its contents. Ask yourself if it is time for an upgrade.
- Next time it suits your budget, invest in some pretty and inspiring intimates.
- Take a moment now and then to admire yourself in your full-length mirror with your lovely underwear on.
- Have a bra fitting done at a local boutique or take your measurements and use an online resource to calculate your bra size.
- Clean out and organize your underwear drawer each season, discarding anything that is worn out and far past its prime.
- Consider the state of your pajamas and loungewear. Put some effort into finding pieces that will elevate the time you spend relaxing.
- Share your wish list with loved ones for holidays and special occasions. Loungewear, pajamas and lingerie make wonderful gifts to give and receive!

# 17

# QUIT ACTING YOUR AGE

How old do you feel? Does the number that just popped into your head match your chronological age? How old you *feel* is much more relevant than the number on the calendar. Looking after your health and embracing all the magic and adventure that life has to offer keeps you feeling young in both body and spirit. I am fortunate to have a number of role models in my life who choose not to "act their age". All of these individuals are in their late seventies or early eighties and are shining, inspiring examples of how to age with vitality. Sure, there are lots of Hollywood stars that look jaw-droppingly gorgeous for their age (J Lo!), but I prefer to seek out real life examples of people thriving in their later seasons of life. I look to my personal mentors for inspiration and motivation in my quest for longevity.

One consistency among my role models is an active lifestyle. They have been active all their lives and have remained active throughout their golden years. Our Dutch neighbours, who are in their eighties, are always on the go! I see the husband cycling everyday through our community. In the winter, he speedskates competitively. His wife maintains a garden that rivals anything I have seen in a magazine or Pinterest! This passion is a labour of love for her, but also a wonderful way to maintain her strength and fitness level. Several years ago, she was in a terrible motor vehicle accident. Riding her bicycle, she was stuck by a car and suffered extensive injuries including many broken bones and even a broken neck. At the time, she was in her mid-seventies. She made a miraculous recovery, which I can only suspect is a result of her strong level of physical fitness. Would you believe she got back on that bicycle? She is an amazing, determined individual. Many people would have been knocked out for life by the injuries she suffered. Her story is such a good reminder why staying active isn't just about trimming your waist and looking good in that dress.

A positive mindset and can-do attitude are also a common theme I have noticed. I have seen so many older people who seem to throw in the towel and give up on life. They tell themselves stories like, "I'm too old for that". Instead of adapting or being creative when faced with a challenge such as a health crisis, they throw their hands up in defeat. Obviously, our physical bodies and capabilities are going to experience decline as each decade passes, but that's not to say we can't keep moving forward! Being open to new adventures and learning experiences keeps you fresh and current at any age.

My father is eighty-two, but he possesses the boyish mindset of an adventurer that keeps him young in both heart and mind. He is always learning and challenging himself with new schemes and endeavours. He has built three airplanes, a sailboat, a pick-up truck and many other miscellaneous projects over the years. When I was twenty-three years old, we bicycled across North America together. He was fifty-eight at the time. We turned a lot of heads that summer on the road. People were quite fascinated by our father/daughter duo. I'm pretty certain I wasn't the point of interest, but rather the "old man" sporting white hair and spandex. I have to be honest, at the time it was no surprise to me that he jumped at the chance to tag along on my dream trip. This was just the dad I knew and loved, always game for something new. (In fact if I asked him to do it all over again today, he would likely say yes!) We were not experienced cyclists with all the latest gear and gadgets. We completed our trek on cheap bicycles from the local hardware store! Despite our lack of equipment and experience, we charged full steam ahead, learning and adapting as we went. Just last year, at the age of eighty-one, he took me on a cycling trip to Croatia with him. Over twenty years later he is still turning heads! He is still the white-haired guy in spandex and was the sole octogenarian in the group! He inspires me to embrace life-long learning and try new things, no matter your age.

My sweet mother is one of those people who radiates vitality. She is just a tiny woman, but she's got a lot of spunk in her step. I love her open-mindedness in the kitchen. She is constantly researching the latest health foods and concocting exotic and healthy recipes. Instead of plodding along with the meat and potatoes diet of the past, she is willing to expand her outlook on nutrition and her culinary skills. She has adopted a similar approach with her wardrobe and general appearance. She is not shy to try new things and update her look, which keeps her looking fresh and modern. She is close to eighty years old and rocks her skinny jeans just as well as a girl in her twenties! She is a great reminder that no matter your age, being open minded and staying current (whether in health, fashion or technology) keeps you fresh and engaged in the world around you.

On the flipside, not acting your age is something to consider for those in younger age categories. If I could write a letter to my younger self, there are so many areas I would advise her to reconsider. The pressure to fit in and follow the crowd during youth is very strong. Of course, hindsight is 20/20, so it is easy for me to look back and recognize my regrets and mistakes. Perhaps you are in your twenties and are finding yourself surrounded by immaturity. Why not raise the bar for yourself and take on a more mature, wiser mindset than most of your peers? Elevating your outlook and actions might just land you that great job you have been searching for. Maybe you will find a like-minded mate. Setting yourself up with good habits at an early age can lead you down a path of wellness and health that will serve you well throughout your life. Instead of living off pizza and beer in university, I could have put a lot more effort into my diet. Maybe then I would not have suffered through years of chronic throat infections and endless consecutive rounds of antibiotics.

In twenty or thirty years from now, what advice will I want to hand down to the woman in her mid-life? No matter your stage in life, it is always a good idea to take a bit of time to reflect on your current situation with an objective state of mind. Can you step back and take an independent look at your current mindset or habits? Even though everyone your age is acting in the same manner, ask yourself if it is possible to take a different path. Herd mentality is an easy thing to fall into without being aware.

If you are particularly interested in the topic of longevity, I recommend reading *The Blue Zones: 9 Lessons for Living Longer from the People Who've Lived the Longest* by Dan Buettner. It explores the habits and actions of those living in regions of the globe with a high incidence of centenarians, and reveals the lifestyle secrets that lead to living a long and healthy life.

My father has a favorite country music song called *The Road Goes on Forever* written by Robert Earl Keen and performed by the Highwaymen. I'm not a huge country music fan myself, but I appreciate the song's message that the party of life never ends. My father parties on, even as he ages. Someday when his last candle goes out, I realize the celebration will continue! He has passed down his zest for life to his children and grandchildren who will keep the party going!

## **ELEVATING ACTIONS:**

- Seek out real life mentors who are aging with vitality. Find inspiration and motivation by observing their actions, behaviours and ways of thinking.
- Don't allow the number on the calendar to dictate how you behave! Keep an open mind and be willing to try new things that challenge you both physically and mentally. Adopt a personal philosophy that embraces lifelong learning and adventure!
- Keep your body moving throughout life. As you encounter physical limits and challenges, seek out creative ways to adjust your activities instead of throwing in the towel.
- Updating your wardrobe now and then with a modern piece can keep you looking and feeling fresh and current. Don't be shy to try a new hairstyle or fashion trend.

- Stay current and informed about the world around you on topics ranging from health, fitness, style, technology, and current events. Keep an open and fresh mindset.
- Check in with yourself regularly to reflect on your current situation in life. Are you following along with the rest of the pack? Are you justifying your actions with the fact everyone else is doing it? Ask yourself if you might benefit from a more productive, uplifting path.

# 18

# STOP PEERING OVER THE FENCE

This next chapter is a letter to myself because admittedly, it is an area I struggle with. In my case, I'm not peering over the other side of the fence, but rather the other side of "the pond". I am a Canadian girl, born and bred. I grew up on the East Coast of Canada in a very small community. I now live seven hundred kilometres from my childhood home, in the province of Nova Scotia. I know I am very fortunate to call Canada my home. I live in a beautiful, majestic country where I feel safe. My house overlooks the stunning (sometimes moody) Atlantic Ocean. My parents and sister reside just a short drive away, and I can visit with them as often as I like. The truth is, I love my life in Canada and feel lucky and blessed to live here. Why then, do I often find myself dreaming longingly of a European lifestyle, complete with ancient stone walls, quaint cafés and freshly baked baguettes?

The first time I visited Europe I was nineteen years old and signed up for a summer student work abroad program. I remember landing in Amsterdam and being completely enthralled by the sights before me: the intricate architecture, charming bicycles, beautiful canals and overflowing flower markets. It was a feast for the senses for a Canadian girl who grew up in a mill town in Northern New Brunswick. I was smitten to say the least. My next stop was Paris, then off to Nice. I eventually ended up on the tiny Greek island of Naxos, where my English-speaking skills were highly attractive to employers. I spent my days selling ferry tickets at the local tourist office, gazing at the brilliant white-washed buildings, cascading flowers and sparkling emerald, Aegean Sea. My life felt truly enchanted to be surrounded by such visual splendour each day. I tried to soak in every last drop of beauty and sunshine. (I should have been wearing sunscreen!)

Since that summer backpacking, I have travelled to Europe a number of times. France is my destination of choice. I am a country mouse, so my visits to Paris have always been a bit of a whirlwind and have never lasted more than two or three days. My "happy place" is the French countryside. I could park myself on an ancient stone wall and happily spend the day people watching and soaking in the Mediterranean sun. The quaint villages, the enchanted forest trails, the pastoral scenes, the abundant and overflowing markets all fill me to the brim with awe and joy.

France is also a destination I love because I speak French and enjoy the opportunity to revisit my language skills. I grew up in a bilingual (French/English) community and attended school in a French immersion program. It feels exotic and exciting to speak the language when in France and converse with the locals. The French are always so kind and patient with me, and being able to communicate with them gives me a better taste of the culture. Why doesn't it feel the same when I speak French at the supermarket or gas station each summer when we head back home to the cottage?

Of course, it is human nature to want what we don't have. I sometimes come back from my trips feeling deflated by my hometown surroundings, which really isn't the purpose of a vacation is it? I am working on finding ways to incorporate a bit of "Euro-chic" into my days. Even just a tiny drop now and then can elevate my mood. I try to turn it into a challenge, or a treasure hunt of sorts, to add a bit of mystery and excitement.

Food is my number one complaint about the North-American culture and it is at the top of my list of what I enjoy when travelling. During my daily outings I am surrounded and bombarded by a generic landscape of big box supermarkets and ubiquitous fast food chains. If I am seeking really fresh, high quality food, I simply have to go out of my way to access it. I still shop at the giant supermarket, but I also take extra steps to seek out higher quality items. I have my greens delivered weekly to my house by a local farm. I travel to a farmer's market as often as I can. I drive to a bakery for my bread (but I have to stock up and freeze my loaves instead of enjoying fresh baked bread each day). The fast food stops are never a consideration. I eat out infrequently, but when I do, I choose one of my favorite local restaurants. I would rather pack a healthy snack than pull up to a drive thru window. Every now and then I find a diamond in the rough. I was digging through the deli case at my giant super market and was shocked to find the exact camembert my Airbnb host referred to as "Le Roi du Fromage". Who knew, it had been hiding there all along, a prize waiting to be discovered?

Maybe you already live the Euro-chic life. If this is the case, I envy you! I imagine you appreciate the access to and availability of a bounty of fresh foods. If your reality is closer to mine, I encourage you to embark on your own treasure-hunting adventure in your local community. It can be expensive to shop at specialty stores, so perhaps pick and choose the items you want to splurge on. Bread and veggies are the two main splurge-worthy items on my shopping list. Check out the international and deli sections of your local supermarket. I was shocked at the selection once I started digging around.

Foreign languages have an exotic appeal to them. I notice that when I am visiting a far-off land, I sometimes prefer to be surrounded by people whom I don't understand! I can sit in a café and daydream without having my head space invaded by the person speaking loudly next to me. If I can't understand them, then it is not possible to involuntarily eavesdrop! I am always amazed when I travel to other parts of the world by the fact that other cultures speak so many different languages. I feel fortunate to have learned French at a young age, but I have definitely gone years where I never uttered a word. I speak from experience, if you don't use it, you lose it!

Over the last five years I have been dusting the cobwebs off my brain cells. The more I work on my French skills, the more confident I feel. Why not do the same with your language of choice? Maybe you have been dreaming of learning Italian. There is no time like the present to dive in, even if a trip to Italy is but a dream on your bucket list. Online resources are abundant, and many cities and towns have conversational meet up groups where you can practice a language live and in person! Living in Canada, we do have French television and radio at our fingertips. When I am in the car, and want a news update, I often tune into the French station instead of the English. I love watching French movies, turning off the subtitles to ensure I am challenging myself. One of my sons has been in a French immersion program at school for the last ten years, so I have been helping him with homework since kindergarten. Staying on top of my French language skills allows me to sprinkle a little Eurochic throughout my day on a regular basis.

People-watching in France is one of my favorite activities. This alone could keep me occupied all day. I always keep a small journal in my handbag and take notes of interesting style combinations or droplets of inspiration I come across. My people-watching episodes at home usually involve being parked outside a junior high school waiting for my sons and checking out what the teens of society are wearing these days. I will admit, I have yet to open my journal to jot down their style tips. (My forty-five-year-old self does not feel the need to showcase her abs!) I turn to the virtual world for inspiration in this department and maintain a number of boards on Pinterest to track style ideas, and just admire pretty pictures! My boards include French country bedroom, Mediterranean meals, Provençal garden inspiration and French girl fashion. When I am in need of a boost, this collection of visuals is there to inspire me. Most people are already using Pinterest, but if you aren't, I encourage you to open an account and start pinning away! I liken it to a form of window shopping. It is a way to just admire the beauty of an image, without necessarily needing or wanting it. Just appreciating it is often enough.

If there is one thing most people will agree on, European style is something to be admired! I think a lot of North American women struggle pulling off the "je ne sais quoi" look because we spent our youth roaming generic shopping malls. I for one was not exposed to any fashion growing up other than the mannequins at the local mall and the pages of *Seventeen* magazine. If you grew up in a big city, your experiences, no doubt, differ a lot from mine!

That first trip to Europe was certainly eye-opening for my nineteen-year-old self. My personal style at the time would have been classified as, "lumberjack chic". I attended Acadia University and I was obviously drawing inspiration from our school mascot, *The Axeman*. I assure you, I was not alone. We all donned Birkenstocks, wool socks, baggy ripped jeans and plaid shirts. Our backpacks were usually adorned with enough climbing rope and carabiners to scale Yosemite's El Capitan (never mind the fact we were just walking to class). My favorite pants at the time were a pair of sweats with "Kiss my Axe" inscribed on the seat. I kid you not!

While my people-watching and style notes were not taken in the high fashion world of Paris, I do notice a difference in the way French women dress in the more rural areas. Style in the South of France is relaxed and casual, yet sophisticated. My vacations have never been shopping trips, but I always find the time to steal away into a few cute boutiques while my boys indulge in gelato. Most often I am not there to purchase, but rather admire and soak up inspiration.

Back home in Canada, I use Instagram to study the aesthetic of European brands. Most of my favorites are certainly not available at my local mall, and ordering from Europe is cost prohibitive. I often turn to eBay to seek out unique items on a budget that I cannot buy locally. My treasure hunting has often allowed me to find certain brands on Canadian soil. In fact, my favorite local boutique now carries Des Petits Hauts and Veja sneakers. I was able to order my pair of Aigle rubber boots from an online store based in Montreal. If you too are craving a bit more Euro-chic flare in your wardrobe, bypass the mall and spend a bit of time treasure hunting for unique, harder to find items in local boutiques, consignment stores or online sites such as eBay.

Unequivocally, the best part of travelling in Europe is the ability to admire the stunning architecture, art and ancient treasures. Unfortunately, this one is pretty much impossible for me to tap into while on Canadian soil. Most of our vacation time in France was spent hiking. The natural beauty on these hikes was stunning, but so was the fact that at every turn we might be pleasantly treated to some ancient piece of history: old caves, crumbling castles, stone walls, Roman ruins. The forests were enchanting and left me yearning for more. In this case, I need to step back and certainly be thankful that I was able to witness these sights. I need to start taking stock of the natural beauty my own country has to offer, and yes, it is outstanding! So, while there are no castle ruins hiding in my forest, there is an untouched beauty that surrounds me. I have access to true nature at my doorstep.

Start taking inventory of all the gifts and unique treasures your own country and community have to offer. When I am overseas and I encounter someone who has visited Canada, I love to ask them what they enjoyed most about my homeland. They remind me of the space, the friendly people and the natural beauty. It's nice to hear that others are peeking over to my side of the fence too!

## ELEVATING ACTIONS:

- If you find yourself longing for aspects of a different culture, seek out ways to infuse a bit of foreign vibe into your day to day life. Send yourself on a treasure hunt to source foods or experiences that are available to you locally.
- Prioritize what parts of the culture you would like to incorporate into your life and make a list of "splurge worthy" items.
- If you speak a foreign language, or wish to learn one, dive in and just do it! The only way to improve or maintain your skills is to engage in the language. Seek out opportunities to both listen and speak.
- Use sites like Pinterest and Instagram to stay connected with images from foreign lands that inspire you.
- Follow clothing brands that may not necessarily be available for purchase in your location and take note of how garments are styled. Seek out creative

ways to acquire special and unique items by scouring consignment stores, specialty boutiques and online resources.
- Remind yourself of all the wonderful aspects of the culture and community you live in. Next time you encounter a tourist, ask them what they are enjoying about their visit. Let their comments serve as reminders for how fortunate you are to live where you do!

# 19

# POWER YOURSELF WITH FINANCIAL INFORMATION

I need to warn you right off the bat, being a professional accountant, the topic of finances is something I can get a bit carried away with! I was the kid who maintained a ledger tracking all deposits and withdrawals from my piggy bank. Needless to say, it is a topic I'm passionate about!

Until I write my next book, I am limiting myself to just one chapter on this topic! I am going to stick to the areas I believe apply to everyone and are of great importance. We are all facing different financial situations and stages of life. Some of you may be in a debt-reduction mode where you are trying to get control of loan balances and pay them off as quickly as possible. Others may find themselves in a stage where their focus is on building wealth and saving for children's education and/or retirement. Perhaps you are entering your golden years and are hoping to stretch your savings. I have a couple of philosophies on the subject of personal finance that will serve you well, regardless of your situation.

Information is power! With some effort and the adoption of regular habits, this power is within your reach and is accessible to all. In order to make wise financial decisions in life, you need to know where you stand. You need to know what you *own, owe, earn* and *spend*. I believe a lot of people feel anxious about their finances, and therefore like to avoid the topic and bury their heads in the sand. Honestly, the more you avoid facing your financial situation, the more heavily it will weigh on your shoulders. Free yourself of this weight by educating and informing yourself.

I am shocked that our education system does not include more instruction on this very important topic that affects absolutely everyone. My son is entering high school next year and is in the process of choosing courses. Since he is planning on attending university, he chose the academic math course. Sadly, the topic of personal finance is only covered in the non-academic math. This makes no sense!

It is not a complicated exercise to sit down with a pen and paper or a spreadsheet and take an inventory of your assets and your debts (including mortgage, car loans, student loans, lines of credit and credit card balances). I suggest you seek advice from a professional financial adviser if you find yourself in a situation where your debt load is heavy and overwhelming. I am not going to delve into the topic of debt-reduction strategies here. (This topic is starting to feel like a future book as well.) Tallying up your household "balance sheet" is an important and often eye-opening experience for many. If you don't know where you stand financially, I recommend really diving in and taking control of the situation, with the help of experts if you need it.

The next piece of advice involves a bit more effort, but this is a very important area that many people overlook. We all have good intentions with budgets. How many times have you thoughtfully drawn up a budget, only to toss it aside when lured astray by the many temptations we face each day? My husband and I draw up an annual budget for the upcoming year just as the current year draws to a close. This is often how we celebrate New Year's Eve! (This is a lot more fun than it sounds. We are both accountants, so it is a sick form of play.) Our numbers are based on what we expect to earn and spend in a year; relying heavily on the prior year information. (See how powerful tracking this information can be?) I then break the annual figures down by month, and pop everything into a spreadsheet.

If you are going to stay on top of your budget, you need to track what you spend! There is no way around this. You cannot make smart and informed purchase decisions if you don't know where you stand. Perhaps you see a perfect dress in the window of your favorite boutique but aren't sure where you sit with your clothing budget this month. Do you go ahead and buy the dress anyway, or do you consider your budget and the commitment you made to yourself and your household? Maybe you had an emergency with the dishwasher this month and overspent on household repairs out of necessity. Is there another discretionary area in your monthly budget you can steal from to cover this unexpected cost? Again, without timely information on your spending activities, you are powerless in your decisions.

Tracking your expenditures has never been easier, since so many of us pay for purchases using electronic means. The banks do all the hard work for us by recording our expenses in the form of bank statements and credit card statements. There are a number of apps and programs available that allow you to simply download your information and produce reports with a click of the mouse. If this intimidates you, Excel spreadsheets or an old-fashioned ledger approach will still assist you in tracking the information you need. I personally use a program called Quicken. It is a very simple exercise to hit "download" each day. Keeping on top of this task and downloading every day ensures my information is current and up-to-date. By doing this task in small chucks, the overall effort feels minimal and manageable. Daily might be a bit extreme for some people, so perhaps a weekly update on Sunday evenings might be a realistic approach for you. I include my daily bank update on my to-do list. Ensuring this task is completed each day gives me a feeling of comfort that I am in control of our spending. The action elevates me and reduces my stress levels!

The next piece of advice comes from the ever so elegant and chic Coco Chanel, "Elegance is refusal". Most of us have heard this quote before, but perhaps have applied it to the concept of dressing and personal style. The act of refusal is also very elegant within the context of developing a healthy financial mindset and habits. It is not elegant to finance all the beautiful things in life by dumping them on your credit card or line of credit. Living within our means and choosing what we bring into our lives carefully is the ultimate form of elegance. Keep this quote in your back pocket next time you are faced with a temptation you are literally drooling over. If it fits within your budget, then certainly, purchasing the item can be up for consideration. If it doesn't fit within your budget, exercise your elegance and admire it from afar! You will be lifted by your sense of self-discipline and the ability to work towards your goals.

All this talk of budgets and spreadsheets might sound boring and deflating, but I can assure you, being in control of your finances is powerful and uplifting! It provides a sense of comfort and peace to know you are in control, informed and headed on the path to reach your goals.

## **ELEVATING ACTIONS:**

- If you have been avoiding the topic of personal finances, take the plunge and get informed about your financial situation, compiling information on what you own, owe, earn and spend.
- Seek advice and assistance from a personal financial planner if you are feeling overwhelmed or unsure on how to proceed. My husband and I are both accountants and we still obtain the advice of professionals.
- Create a budget for your household and actually stick to it!
- Track your expenditures regularly so that you can make informed decisions in a timely manner.
- Live within your means and your budget. Exercise restraint when faced with temptations that do not fit with your financial goals. Feel pride in staying focused on your goals and elegantly refusing temptation!

# 20

# REVISIT PAST PASSIONS

We all experience times in our lives when we feel a bit stale and uninspired. Maybe you find yourself in this position at the moment. Perhaps you feel like you are plodding along aimlessly and have lost your zest and enthusiasm for life. Maybe it is time to reignite that fire inside you, as no doubt the embers are still there, they just need a little stir.

I too have found myself in this position (quite recently). I think it is just part of the natural up and down nature of life and an effect of the pressures and stressors that go hand in hand with each season. I found myself feeling a bit stale and bored with my activities and routines and was seeking something that would ignite a bit of passion and enthusiasm inside me. I knew I needed to tap into *something*, but I just didn't know what that *something* was. It took a bit of trial and error, but I eventually found myself back on track and the results are in your hands.

*This book* is the product of my search to rediscover and engage in a passion from my past.

We often hear advice to refrain from dwelling on the past. While I agree there is no point in beating yourself up over previous mistakes and behaviours, I do believe reflecting on the past certainly offers an opportunity to learn and gain insight into what makes you tick. Obviously, we all grow and evolve as we journey through life. What I have found is that some past habits and behaviours are best left in the past! The fact that we eliminated them from our lives is indeed positive. Others, however, may have been sadly forgotten or lost in the flurry of our lives.

Reconnecting with the person you were before and revisiting prior passions may reignite an old flame that has been smoldering in the background. Perhaps you spent your summers riding horses as a child. Your busy life working full-time and ferrying your kids to their activities has caused you to forget this past love. You have not stepped foot in a stable for decades. Identifying this past passion might lead you back to it with a bit of creativity. Maybe instead of your weekly run club meet up, you could spend your Saturday mornings in a riding lesson doing something you find much more uplifting than pounding the pavement. Perhaps just taking a Sunday drive through the countryside and stopping to pet a few warm, velvety muzzles through a fence would be enough fill your soul with a bit of pleasure.

I walked myself through a number of exercises in an effort to reconnect with the piece of myself I felt had gone missing somewhere along the way. I decided to dust off some cobwebs and awaken the little girl inside me. Childhood can be a wonderful place to mentally time travel. As children, we are not yet burdened by the responsibilities of adulthood, so our focus in life is play. Tapping into your former forms of play and what you did for leisure time in your youth is a powerful method to stir the coals. I grabbed a journal and made a list of the first things that popped in my head when reflecting on my younger self. Here is what I came up with :

Crafts

Reading

My pet beagle

Berry picking

Beachcombing

Lilacs and forget-me-nots

Bouquets of wildflowers

Nostalgic 1970's style on my cute mother

Tap dancing

Broadway musical songs

Climbing trees

Zooming around on my red bicycle

Piling firewood with my dad in a wool sweater

This list appears random, but using it as a base for inspiration allowed me to identify my "likes" and integrate them into my current life in small but meaningful ways: gathering a bouquet of wildflowers for the dinner table, going blueberry picking with my mother, finally planting a lilac bush in the backyard, buying that cute one-piece jumpsuit for my summer wardrobe, downloading the Annie soundtrack and blasting it in the car while singing along at the top of my lungs. Each of these small actions connected me with my true self and served to elevate my life. This list actually gave me the final push I needed to adopt my little toy poodle Coco! Fondly remembering our family dog growing up made me realize just how much joy and love he brought to our lives. (My father would likely argue that his beagle nose and desire to roam added a lot of frustration!) Coco is probably the best thing that has ever happened to our family!

Identifying my love of reading also reminded me of how much time I spent as a child with my nose in a book. I could often be found reading or writing in my diary. Writing letters to myself always served as a therapeutic tool that enabled me to really dissect and gain a deeper understanding of my feelings. As a new mother, I maintained a blog where I chronicled my adventures staying home raising my babies. At the time, I had a passion for natural parenting, toy making and creating a home environment that encompassed the Montessori philosophy of learning. I really enjoyed expressing myself in written form and connecting with other like-minded individuals who shared my interests. The kids, of course, grew into tweens then teens and this area of my life became a part of my past. Identifying my former passion for books and writing lead me directly to where I sit today; at my computer, working on my first book!

What does your list look like? I really encourage you to give this exercise a try. You might be pleasantly surprised with what your brain unearths from the past. If you are having a hard time coming up with a list, try pulling out some of your old childhood photo albums. The visual cues of your toothy grin back then may bring back some long-lost memories. Another way to connect with your childhood is to physically return to your old stomping grounds. I realize this might not be possible for a lot of people, but if the opportunity exists, why not take advantage of it? Perhaps your parents still live in your childhood home. Daydreaming in your old bedroom, or walking down the street you played hopscotch on, can flood your mind with recollections. My parents moved away from my hometown long ago, but they now live close to my university town. I sometimes walk through the old campus and reminisce about that young naïve girl with big dreams and Birkenstock sandals! I also visit the family cottage every summer. Walking the same sandbars I did as a child is a very grounding experience for me.

Sit down with family members or call an old childhood friend. Everyone loves to reminisce about funny stories from the past. The people who have known you all your life might be the best ones to help you rediscover what you may have lost.

Sometimes this process works and sometimes it does not, but you won't know until you give it a try. Certainly, there are times that taking a plunge and trying something new and out of your comfort zone is the answer to adding spark to your life. Other times, the answer has been inside you all along, you just didn't know it.

## **ELEVATING ACTIONS:**

- Consider former passions that may warrant revisiting. They just might hold the secret to that special something that is missing in your life.
- Take yourself on a time-travel adventure down memory lane. Make a list of everything that pops into your head about your childhood. Let the words flow freely and at random.
- Peruse through old family photos to help remind yourself of the child you once were and what made you smile back then.
- Visit your old stomping grounds. Walk the streets and paths you did as a child. Lie on your old single bed and stare up at the ceiling, losing yourself in thought.
- Have fun reminiscing about old stories with your family and friends from the past. These special

people might see something you are unable to identify in yourself.
- Be creative with incorporating past passions into your current life. If there's a will, there's a way!

# 21

# FIND MAGIC IN MAINTENANCE

The other day I was scrubbing our hardwood floors and found myself being transported back to the summer days of my youth. I had splashed a cap full of Murphy's oil soap into my cleaning bucket, and its nostalgic scent flooded me with fond memories. Back in my equestrian days, one of my favorite activities was caring for the riding tack, which included all the leather accessories such as the saddle and bridle. In preparation for our summer's end horse show, we would gather all our equipment on the farm's driveway and spend a sunny afternoon scrubbing and polishing our leather gear to a brilliant shine. I always looked forward to this day. There was something so satisfying in transforming the dusty, grimy leather into a state of beauty. Murphy's oil soap was a staple in the tack room, and though my riding days are long behind me, I still reach for this product in the grocery aisle. (Gosh, this sounds like an advertisement!) Each time I pull out the mop and bucket, my home is filled with that familiar, comforting scent. It is a small act that adds an elevating touch of magic to my weekly chores.

Do the words cleaning, scrubbing, housework and laundry fill you with dread? Properly caring for our home and personal belongings can actually be a rewarding activity if we approach it with the right mindset. I never viewed washing those saddles as a chore, but rather an experience that enhanced my appreciation for the object and the service it provided. Bringing it back to life and restoring its luster was in essence, an act of gratitude. We live in such a disposable culture, with a heavy focus on replacing instead of repairing and maintaining. Thankfully, I do see small shifts in this societal mindset happening. Caring for our belongings is beneficial to our planet and uplifting to our finances.

Over the years I have compiled a wardrobe of beautiful garments that I really appreciate wearing and admiring. I purchased each item with great thought and consideration, with the intention of enjoying them for many years to come. Obviously, I invested money in these pieces, so I want to ensure each garment lives to its full potential.

I realize the word laundry doesn't exactly spark a great deal of excitement in most people. I do actually *enjoy* caring for my finer pieces of clothing. I keep a separate little laundry basket in my closet for my personal delicate items. These special pieces are kept far away from the family laundry hamper! Getting lost amongst the mountains of stinky t-shirts and muddy jeans would spell disaster. I usually tackle a couple of loads of handwashing a week. I wash all my underwear, sleepwear, sweaters, t-shirts and blouses by hand. For most items, I use a line of soaps from a company called Soak that are pleasantly scented. For my woolens, I use a product called Eucalan. Studier garments, such a jeans, are washed inside out on the delicate cycle (cold water) of my front load washer. Depending on the item, I might take the extra step to place it in a mesh laundry bag. All of my personal laundry is hung or laid flat to dry. It sounds like a lot of work to wash t-shirts by hand, but this extra bit of effort really does make a significant difference in extending the life of your wardrobe. The rest of my clothing, such as workout wear and socks, is tossed in the family laundry bin.

Staying on top of little maintenance issues elevates your wardrobe by keeping garments looking polished and fresh. My maintenance arsenal includes a sewing kit, lint brush, sweater shaver, lavender and cedar sachets and a small spray bottle of vodka. Why not compile your own little toolkit so you are well-prepared when maintenance issues arise? Store it somewhere handy like your closet so you don't find yourself rummaging through a junk drawer before you can sew on that button. Tending to little issues regularly helps the task feel manageable.

This upkeep makes a huge difference over the long run. Tending to lint and pilling on a regular basis really keeps your sweaters, coats and jackets looking crisp and new. I use vodka spray to freshen up the interior of my woolen coats and jackets since these are only dry cleaned once a year. I tuck lavender and cedar sachets in my sweater drawer to keep moths and unpleasant odors at bay.

It does not take long for footwear to get grimy! I keep a stash of shoe care products in our entryway closet to inspire me to perform regular maintenance on my beloved collection of shoes and boots. I am definitely more conscientious in the winter months, ensuring I wipe down my leather boots daily to clear them of damaging salt residue. I use a variety of conditioning and weather-proofing products to protect all my leather footwear from the elements. Prior to retiring them to storage in the off season, I always do a thorough cleaning and conditioning before slipping them back into their original boxes. (Yes, I keep them all!) Storing your unused footwear in dust covers or boxes is an important step in keeping them clean and fresh.

I have a few shoes with unique needs that I handle a bit differently. I am a huge fan of Swedish Hasbeens wooden clogs. I treat these special beauties with a gentle touch of fine sandpaper to wipe off scuffs, followed by a nourishing dose of olive oil. My white leather Veja sneakers are my biggest challenge! I remove the laces and soak them in stain remover a couple of times a season. My secret to keeping the white leather gleaming is the Mr. Clean Magic Eraser. It really does work magic on dark scuffs or stains on white leather as long as you are sure to use a gentle touch. (Again, I realize I sound like a cleaning product advertisement!)

Do you have special, delicate items in your wardrobe and home that require a gentler hand? I am most certain that you do! It is a good idea to read fabric care labels *before* you purchase a garment. You should know what you are getting yourself into before laying down your hard-earned cash. If you are someone who doesn't hold a great track record for taking care of your belongings, you might want to stick to purchasing items that are sturdier in nature and require less attentive maintenance. Alternatively, may I suggest you shift your mindset and come to view the care of your belongings as an enjoyable activity, instead of a dreaded chore.

Perhaps you received a stunning handmade cutting board as a wedding gift. Why not pull out the lovely scented beeswax polish that came with it? Find pleasure in carefully polishing the wood and admiring its rich patina, while breathing in the honey scent of the wax. Describing the scene in this fashion makes the "chore" of waxing the board sound quite dreamy and alluring, doesn't it? Could you approach your other maintenance activities with the same mindset? As you wash your pretty lace and silk intimates by hand, can you enjoy the soothing feel of the warm water and the relaxing scent of the lavender detergent?

Of course, not all the items in our lives are "pretty". Staying on top of the regular upkeep of all your belongings (glamourous or not) is still extremely important! It is likely that the most expensive items in your life fall into the less glamourous category! Your vehicle is an obvious item where regular maintenance can certainly save you gobs of money over the long run. Both our family cars are undercoated each year to ward off rust. This is not an exciting chore by any stretch, but I do take pride in checking it off my to-do list each fall! I keep a list and schedule of all household maintenance tasks in my to-do list binder and check in regularly to see what is coming up on the agenda. This includes anything from having the chimney swept, to the septic pumped (so not glamorous)!

## **ELEVATING ACTIONS:**

- Adopt the mindset that caring for your belongings properly is an act of gratitude, frugality and respect.
- Read the care instructions of an item before you purchase it to ensure you are willing and able to look after it properly.
- Designate a separate laundry basket for your delicates to prevent them from ending up in the washing machine inadvertently.

- Pick up nicely scented detergents and cleaning products that will make your cleaning chores a bit more enjoyable.
- Before storing off-season items, take the time to clean them and tidy up any maintenance issues. Store items in boxes or dust bags to keep them fresh and clean while not in use.
- Create a tool kit of items used to perform tiny wardrobe repairs. Store it in a convenient location so it is on hand when needed.
- Create a maintenance list and schedule (annual and monthly) for all household systems, appliances, structures and vehicles.

# 22

## ACT NOW

As I prepare to sign off, I would like to leave you with one last nibble of food for thought. Daydreams, reflections, to-do lists and diary entries all represent wonderful tools in the process of improving and elevating our lives, but if they never come to life, they will never serve their full purpose! So, go ahead, grab your notes and lists and act now! Do something, no matter how miniscule, to get the wheels of change in motion.

Not long ago, I found myself in a bit of a slump. Our family was in pandemic lockdown, along with the rest of the world. I was in desperate need of a project to spark some light inside me, but was fumbling along in my search for inspiration. Magically, an email appeared in my inbox from one of my favorite lifestyle authors, Fiona Ferris. She was announcing the release of her most recent book, *The Chic Author*. I have read all of Fiona's books and absolutely adore her style of writing and her view on life. That being said, the first thought that popped in my head was that perhaps her newest title was not for me. I wasn't really planning on becoming an author anytime soon, although I did enjoy the act of writing. I decided to download a sample on my Kindle, and I was hooked after the first paragraph. I finished the book by nightfall, and the next morning I was enthusiastically writing the first chapter of my own manuscript.

As I was making my way through Fiona's book, I encountered a number of mental roadblocks and excuses my own brain was dumping in my path. How could I possibly find time to write? I felt like the walls were closing in on me with everyone home and the kids underfoot. My computer was tied up all day with homeschooling. Sure, I was intrigued and inspired by the idea of becoming an author, but *right now* just didn't seem like a good time. Instead of pulling over to the curb, I decided to carry on with the journey and find solutions to my problems (excuses). Fiona guided me through this process and helped me think outside the box. I started getting up at 4 a.m. so I could write for two full hours in peace and quiet each day. I set some boundaries on the use of the family computer. Once the schoolwork was complete, the boys had to give me time and space to work on my project. Their YouTube video watching would have to wait! My husband even made me a cute "do not disturb" sign to post on our family room door to remind people that I was working. The truth was, *now* wasn't a perfect time to start the book, but *later* would have its own set of challenges as well. Do you have a goal in mind, but find yourself identifying all the reasons you just can't make it happen? Be honest with yourself. Are you making excuses? Would a bit of creativity and flexibility allow you to make adjustments and set you on the path towards achieving your goal? Axing excuses is critical in your quest to elevate your life!

Perhaps the goal itself feels overwhelming. Maybe you have a lot of weight to lose, and just thinking about the effort required to drop that many pounds makes you want to throw in the towel before you even get started. In instances such as this, I suggest shifting your focus away from your end goal. The classic "baby steps" approach will get you moving in the right direction, without the sense of overwhelm.

When my father and I cycled across Canada, we never once pulled out a map of the entire country. We started our journey at "Mile 0" of the Trans-Canada Highway in Victoria, British Columbia. We purchased provincial (and state) maps every time we crossed a border. Each evening we sat down with our map and analyzed the terrain and weather we expected to encounter the following day. This information dictated the next day's route and destination. Approaching the journey with a day-by-day mentality made our goal feel achievable and manageable. We pedaled our way across the country for fifty-six days in total, covering over five thousand kilometers! That statement certainly conveys the fact that we completed a tremendously challenging adventure. Life on the road, however, had a relaxed easiness to it, because of our one pedal at a time mindset. (I will admit certain days in the Rocky Mountains were far from easy, as was sleeping in a tent with my snoring father!)

Perfectionism is another sneaky cousin of excuses and overwhelm. It too can hold us back from taking action in our lives and implementing change. I speak from experience when I say perfectionism can be paralyzing. Have you ever found yourself with a case of "analysis paralysis"? I am a master of pros and cons lists. I sometimes have difficulty making decisions because I have a tendency to overanalyze situations. My desire to make a "perfect" decision can sometimes lead to inaction and missed opportunity. When I was contemplating the purchase of my puppy Coco, I found myself paralyzed. I wanted a fluffy, cuddly ball of love, but the practical side of me was listing all the negatives to dog ownership. I hummed and hawed for days on end. When I finally contacted the breeder to tell him I was going to go ahead with the adoption, he informed me that Coco had been sold! I missed the opportunity! Lucky for me, this story has a happy ending. With provincial border restrictions in place during the Covid-19 pandemic, Coco's new owner was not able to travel to pick him up. The stars aligned and Coco ended up coming home with us. This was a case of pure luck! My perfectionistic tendencies could have easily cost me my beloved little poodle!

Perhaps you dream of having a clean and organized home from top to bottom. Depending on your family and household situation, achieving a home environment that meets your high standards may be very difficult, if not impossible to achieve. With the possibility of a "perfect" home out of reach, you give up and let the whole place fall into a state of disaster. By letting go of perfectionism, you could come to terms with the fact that while a pristine house might not be possible, a *pretty tidy* one might be. A *pretty tidy* home sounds a lot better than a disaster zone. Releasing the grip on perfection and lowering standards a tiny bit can elevate the overall picture.

It's also important to keep in mind that it is exhausting, if not impossible, to keep too many plates spinning at once. I don't pretend to have all areas of my life running perfectly. I have tried to be a granola-making, frugal, fashionable, neat-freak, mindful, healthy-eating, glamorous, six-pack sporting woman, and it doesn't take long for everything to come crashing down. Pace yourself and prioritize your goals and actions for a better life. While I am working on this book, the housekeeping is definitely slipping! At this particular moment, my soul-feeding project is much more important than a freshly scrubbed toilet. Above all else, be kind to yourself!

## **ELEVATING ACTIONS:**

- Pull out your to-do lists and journals and take action today! Find even one small task you can perform that will set you on the path towards achieving your goals.
- Identify excuses for what they are. Approach your goals with a creative and flexible mindset.
- If you find yourself feeling overwhelmed with ambitious plans, break the process down into small bite-sized chunks. Stop focusing on the end product and redirect your attention to the task at hand.
- Release yourself from the constraints of perfectionism. There are times in life when adopting a "good enough" philosophy results in a better end product.
- Be kind to yourself, always!

# A NOTE FROM THE AUTHOR

Thank you so much for reading my book and listening to my observations, opinions and musings on life! I appreciate you taking a chance and clicking "buy" on my first attempt at writing a book. I hope I was successful in providing you with inspiration and motivation to take action and implement a few ideas that will bring more joy, comfort, vitality and peace to your life. The writing process itself actually inspired *me* to reignite my passion for many of the topics I covered, tweaking areas here and there to suit the changing landscape of my life. As I mentioned in the introduction, living well is about the journey, and not the destination. There are always areas for improvement, with new and fresh ideas available to help you achieve your goals.

I would love to continue the conversation of elevating daily life with you! Please feel free to connect with me. You can reach me by email, or on my Instagram page.

jenniferlynnmelville@gmail.com

www.instagram.com/the.elevated.everyday

Much love,

*Jennifer*

## OTHER BOOKS BY JENNIFER MELVILLE

### *Elevate Your Personal Style:*
*Inspiration for the Everyday Woman*

### *Elevate Your Health:*
*Inspiration and Motivation to Embrace and Maintain a Healthy Lifestyle*

### *Elevate Your Life at Home:*
*Inspiring Ideas to Add Joy, Peace and Magic to Your Homelife*

### *Elevate Your Money Mindset:*
*Approach Your Finances with Positivity, Confidence and Enthusiasm*

### *Preloved Chic:*
*Stylish Secrets to Elevate Your Wardrobe With Second-Hand Fashion*

### *Seashells in my Pocket:*
*50 Ways to Live a Beach Inspired Life*

### *Paris in my Panties:*
*Live Your Best (French Inspired) Life*

# ABOUT THE AUTHOR

Jennifer Melville is a self-published author. She decided to take the plunge and write her first book because she wanted to tap into the community of like-minded individuals who share in her enthusiasm for living well and seeking ways to elevate daily life. She is a professional accountant by trade, who approaches life with an analytical and observant mind. Jennifer has been exploring the concept of elevating the everyday for over twenty years. She is passionate about family, health, fitness, fashion, nutrition, nature and all the beauty life has to offer.

Jennifer lives by the sea in beautiful Nova Scotia, Canada with her husband, two sons and toy poodle Coco.

Printed in Great Britain
by Amazon